MindStore

ABOUT THE AUTHOR:

Seven years ago Jack Black was a social worker in the deprived East End of Glasgow. After seeing two colleagues destroy their health through the stress of work whilst only in their 40s, and then experiencing a similar collapse himself, he decided that it was time to change his life.

Working in the areas of stress-management and mental fitness, he set himself the task of developing a British programme of personal development and positive attitude. MindStore was set up in the early 1990s and broke new ground in personal, business and sports motivation. Corporate clients include Glaxo, Allied Dunbar, the Metropolitan Police and Thomas Cook. Jack Black has also worked with numerous sports teams and Olympic athletes.

Thousands of people from all walks of life have benefited from his courses.

MindStore gave my management team creativity, self-belief and the energy to seize the day. ABBEY NATIONAL

MindStore has been helping police officers achieve higher standards of quality and performance. METROPOLITAN POLICE

MindStore achieved exceptionally high ratings from staff at all levels. THE ROBERT GORDON UNIVERSITY

MindStore has given me the toolbox I require to build the life I've always dreamed of. COLIN MURDOCH

The techniques I have learned have brought immense personal happiness, contentment and – most of all – the knowledge that I alone control my life. DOROTHY MACGREGOR

MindStore

The Ultimate Mental Fitness Programme

JACK BLACK

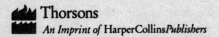
Thorsons
An Imprint of HarperCollins*Publishers*

Thorsons
An Imprint of HarperCollins*Publishers*
77–85 Fulham Palace Road,
Hammersmith, London W6 8JB
1160 Battery Street,
San Francisco, California 94111–1213

Published by Thorsons 1994

10 9 8 7 6 5 4 3 2

© Jack Black 1994

Jack Black asserts the moral right to
be identified as the author of this work

A catalogue record for this book
is available from the British Library

ISBN 0 7225 2994 5

Printed in Great Britain by
HarperCollinsManufacturing Glasgow

To my wonderful partner in life, Norma,
and our two sons Anthony and Christopher
without you how could I possibly achieve anything?

Contents

Acknowledgements

There are many, many people I would like to thank who directly or indirectly have assisted me in developing the MindStore programme and this book itself. I must first thank all who have participated in the countless courses I have taught over the years: by using the MindStore techniques they have been an inspiration to countless others. I owe particular gratitude to my good friend and mentor Jim Bell, without whom there would never have been a MindStore programme. Likewise the MindStore team, especially Cecelia, Carole, Mo, Janet, and Rena. May I also thank Shian for her contribution. Closer to home when I needed that little bit of encouragement, my father Jack Black Sr, and Theresa were always there, as well as Janette and Isobel, who have always helped in the background.

Introduction

There was a time in my life when I was a community worker in Glasgow's East End. I was committed to this work – or at least as committed as I thought then that a person could be.

In a relatively short period of time, however, a whole range of events with profound meaning for me caused me to take stock and reach out for a new life. My wife's mother died suddenly from a stroke (my own mother had died in similar circumstances some years before). Two men who were significant to me in Social Work and Community Education at the highest levels died – one from cancer, the other from heart disease. I was increasingly disillusioned by the feeling of hopelessness in the communities in which I worked. I felt that we had no real strategies for change; indeed I felt we were only working to cover up the cracks.

My career was stuck – I had looked at further promotion but knew I did not really fit in. My salary was such that I seemed to go over budget most months. I took cheap holidays and they were really the only thing I had to look forward to. I was unhappy; I knew there was much more that could be done with my life, but what?

It was my time to change, and by reading personal development books by such people as Norman Vincent Peale and Napoleon Hill I began to realize just how negative I and everyone else around me seemed to be. I had long since lost any significant measure of ambition.

On reflecting on the recent deaths of the people who had been so important to me, I started to wonder about the effects of stress and the impact it could have. I myself was suffering constantly from it. I was an excellent hypochondriac, always at my doctor with silly little complaints which I had magnified in my mind until they had serious negative meanings. I was forever thinking that the twinge in my chest was the start of a heart attack, or that I had cancer.

Unknown to me at that time, my life began to change when I started organizing skiing outings to raise funds for a local youth project. Once their use as fund-raisers was no longer required, a colleague and I continued the trips, thus leading to the start of my first business. I was still working full-time as a community worker and these were not easy times; there was a lot of insecurity. It demanded all my time and more besides. I found myself drifting away from my friends. Instead of socializing I was working almost every hour I had. I knew from the books I'd read that you had to pay the price and stick with it; I somehow knew that by keeping at it I would win through and the hard work would be worthwhile.

On reflection, moving further and further away from my friends to work on my new business was the hardest part. I remember quite clearly I had felt resentful when another friend had set himself up in business some time before and had to spend less time socializing. I suspect I became less popular with close friends when I did this too. Indeed I am convinced that this is one of the issues we must face if we wish to embrace change in our lives.

Later my business had expanded into group travel and I was working all the hours I could on it while at the same time working in one of Glasgow's most deprived areas. All this work soon took its toll and I collapsed one day in the city centre.

This was the turning point. I now knew that I had to do something about my own stress. To cut a long story short, I set out on a journey to find out as much as I could about stress and finally to manage it in my life. This led me to discover wonderful yet simple processes which not only can help you to manage your health and energy but which can be used to transform anybody's life.

What I discovered amazed me and I realized that I wanted to share my new knowledge with everyone. All around me I could only see people who could benefit, especially my close friends and colleagues. The funny thing is that now, years later, having shared my ideas with the country's major companies (both management and staff, at all levels) together with the country's leading sportsmen and -women and indeed thousands of men, women and children every year, I have still yet to attract my friends and colleagues to my courses. Maybe they just cannot believe that I could change so much.

My life has changed. It has changed dramatically over a relatively short time. I have enjoyed being involved with experiences and opportunities that most people only dream about. I am blessed with a wonderful family life, we live in beautiful rural surroundings and I have a lifestyle that I would previously have thought could never be mine. Of course it hasn't been easy – life is not like that – but I have found an inner strength and confidence that have made all the difference. Recently I met Margaret Thatcher and I heard her say that when she took over as leader of the Conservative Party she had a vision for the future. She knew in advance there would be many problems and that she would have to fight her way through them before reaping the benefits of her hard work.

My intention with this book is to provide you with the tools to improve the quality of your life. To bring positive results for your family, your relationships, in your career and business. To help you stretch and grow, to find – if need be – happiness, love and success. What I will share with you I have been presenting to thousands every year through the MindStore courses. I tell you now that it will work for you too. As I always say, *'It Only Works.'* If at this stage you are somewhat sceptical then that is obviously normal, but please bear with me and read on.

There is nothing new in my techniques, they have existed as far back as I can make out – since time began. Perhaps the way I have put them together is different, but that's all. I have attempted to keep it all as simple as possible. My intention is to instruct you in a way of doing things that will bring the improvements you seek in life. I am less concerned about why it all works; there are many who choose to invest in such a study and I leave that to them. I prefer to use tools that will give results to anyone who wishes to learn and apply them. There is really nothing extraordinary about my approach; what *is* extraordinary is that moment when we choose to change and grow.

Believe me, *'It Only Works.'*

What Is MindStore All About?

I find that a simple model can help explain a complex idea in such a way that we can grasp it and then make it work in our lives.

For example, if you picture the conscious and subconscious parts of the human mind as an iceberg, the conscious mind can be represented as the section above the surface of the ocean, while the subconscious is the much larger part below the surface, approximately 7/8ths of the total.

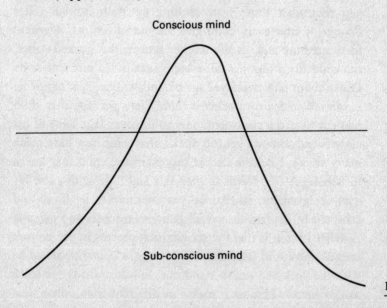

Conscious mind

Sub-conscious mind

The human brain has 20,000 programmes built in at birth. We know how to breathe and digest at birth – indeed, we are born with an insatiable desire for oxygen, food and, perhaps, love. Certainly many would argue that a baby searches for security, comfort and love. I believe this desire for love and acceptance never leaves us.

I know myself that each time I am introduced to an audience to talk about the MindStore Programme, whether it is an audience of thousands or only a handful, I sense the need to be accepted. I always look for that first smile on the face of a listener – only then do I feel comfortable.

I believe that as a child attending your first class at school the desire to be loved and accepted is a vital motivator. My son only recently started his first class and came home in those early days and weeks proudly informing us of his new friends and new experiences. Then come the first school exams – do you remember those little spelling or multiplication tests? Sooner or later every child gets ten out of ten or full marks for something and, as the teacher returns the marked paper, the child finds that his self-esteem soars for a moment as he thinks about how overjoyed his parents will be, how happy he is himself in his own achievement. Then perhaps that child looks around the classroom, only to discover that some of his close friends did not get full marks, that some may have made many errors. I believe that at this point the child first learns to 'sabotage' – he learns to play safe and hide or disguise his own achievement, so that he can continue to be loved and accepted by his friends as well as by his teachers and parents.

What I mean is that the socialization process in our culture creates in most of us, from an early age, a strong desire to be with the pack and not to stand out. In other words, we learn to fear success because it makes us different from others, and we need their love and acceptance.

Success means lots of things to lots of people. For me it is the ability to strive to be the best you can be, at all things you attempt: to be happy, joyous, content, healthy, loving, giving, to achieve and give all you've got in a chosen career, in sport, in love and in relationships – in other words, to stand up and be the person you can be, to give 100 per cent every minute of the day, to seize the day.

I believe that the vast majority of us learn subconsciously to sabotage ourselves so that we can remain safely within our peer group, because if we actually perform better, are happier, more content – indeed achieve much more, then the fear of not being liked takes over and we revert to steering the middle ground rather than reaching higher.

I believe this is a cultural challenge we all face in our lives. You and I both know that there is much, much more we can all achieve, can all contribute, but for some reason we do not or seem unable to take the necessary action.

I recognize that success can mean lots of things. I suppose I see success as someone striving to do better but with a sense of balance in his or her life. On my MindStore courses, participants often cite Anita Roddick, Richard Branson, Mother Theresa, Margaret Thatcher, Linford Christie and Evelyn Glennie as successes who seem to exhibit characteristics such as commitment, motivation, determination, confidence and a sense of vision.

On the other hand, those the participants would describe as being failures exhibit the characteristics of low self-esteem, lack of energy, loneliness, depression, helplessness and indifference.

Recently some of my friends and I found ourselves talking about success. I listened carefully because these friends were not members of MindStore. A number of great sportsmen and

-women, leading businesspeople and people from history were mentioned. In looking for the attributes that stood out, my friends decided that what made the fundamental difference was that in each of these cases the successful person had made an initial decision to achieve whatever it was that he or she did indeed go on to accomplish and for which he or she has become justly well known. That it was this decision, backed up by commitment, that was the essence of success.

For me this is the secret of success, happiness, joy, love and all the other things we strive for. For me it is not complicated or difficult, it is basically simple. *Your thinking determines all things.* In other words, think negatively and you will attract negative realities; think positively and the benefits you desire in life will come to you. It's that simple.

Whatever we choose to think we choose to have in our lives.

In many ways, that's it! The book is finished, you do not really need anything else!

If only it were easy to take this idea to your heart. Yes, it's easy enough to understand intellectually – but taking it to heart, this is the real challenge. If it were easy to accept that our thoughts determine everything, that would be enough. However, we all need some guidelines, some pointers to how to make this concept a way of life. I trust you will find that you can use the simple techniques in this book to make the difference, to bring you instant results and improve how you experience your life – and, hopefully, that this will encourage you to move towards thinking *BIG*, towards really going for it. Let's begin!

2

The First Step

Taking a Look at Your Life

The journey of a thousand miles begins with the first step.

LAO-TSE TUNG

The starting point is to reflect on where you are at this stage in your life. I have found that the little exercise that follows is useful in determining how my life is at any given time, while identifying where things can be improved. I recommend that you take the time right now to do this yourself. It's a good idea to copy what follows onto a separate piece of paper, since it is useful to repeat the exercise after some time has passed, at which point you can reflect on the improvements you have made.

The Wheel of Life

This simple tool can help you to analyse key areas in your life and can provide you with the initial desire to do something about making changes. The idea is to represent your life as a wheel. Life is a journey across the planet and across time. The condition of your wheel will reflect how smooth your journey seems at present.

Draw a large circle on a sheet of paper and divide it off into eight key areas or sections. I am suggesting that there are eight key areas to life, but you can add more if you wish. Further divide each section with another line and hatch it off on a scale of 1 to 10 (see the figure below). The idea here is to give yourself a score for each area of your life. Ten (at the circumference of the wheel) means that everything is absolutely perfect in a given area of your life, while one (at the centre of the wheel) means that this area is, for you, completely dire.

WHEEL OF LIFE

Date. . . . . ,

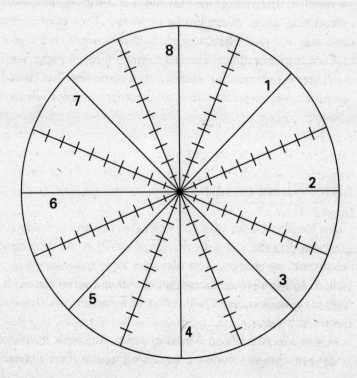

1. FAMILY LIFE

Most of us would agree that family life is important. Culturally a great deal of emphasis is placed on this and we tend to accept that family life should be loving, caring, nurturing, supportive, etc., etc. The reality is that most people I meet find that their family life can provide them with major challenges. At a simple level, a four-month-old baby can keep a colleague awake at night and his or her own mood may be affected. Or a teenage member of the family may be keeping company that is causing considerable concern.

Family life can be a source of great stress in its own right and you can be sure that any challenge that exists within yours will be having an effect elsewhere. It can affect your work, your studies, your relationships and much more besides. To have a family life score of 10, absolutely perfect, is something that is surely worth striving for. The techniques that follow can have a big impact on this area, but let's begin by being honest and plotting the score on a scale of 1 to 10. Whatever family life means for you, then consider that. It can mean a single unit or a more extended family group; you may be living on your own and only visiting your family once a year – whatever family life means to you, give yourself a current score (see the figure overleaf).

2. SOCIAL LIFE

Here I do not necessarily mean how often you go out with friends to enjoy yourself in a nightclub or at social activities. I am really referring to the reality of getting on with other human beings – a vital component of life. We have to relate to so many people: those we work with and live with, those

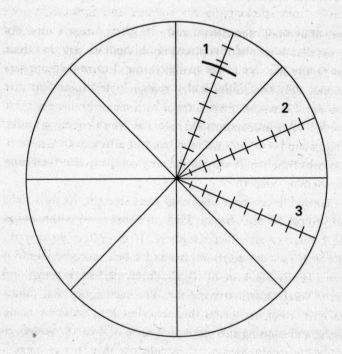

who help us through the check-out at the supermarket, bank tellers, taxi drivers, and so on.

One of my observations from working closely with many successful people is how they seem to be genuinely at ease with anybody they meet. They are able to care about others and respect them. They have a deep inner confidence that helps them to relate to anybody. I have also observed how so many people limit themselves by falling into the trap of looking up to some people and looking down on others. Much of British culture encourages this, but it really does limit and hold people back.

How easy are you in different social situations? Do you refrain from speaking up for yourself and forwarding your contributions to discussions and chit-chat? Do you miss out on opportunities and invitations? I can honestly say that those I have met who are at the so-called top of their field are only human, they don't bite and are usually good fun. So give yourself a mark for your social life: Ten? – You are the life and soul of the party, everyone loves you, you are really popular, you are fully confident yet sensitive and caring to all you meet. One?: Surely not. Such people are locked up for their own protection.

3. PERSONAL DEVELOPMENT

One of my observations of those who truly succeed in life is how they commit themselves continually to learning and improving themselves. Yet there are those with that 'I know it all' attitude, with closed minds, who hold themselves and everyone around them back. Are you a 10: committed to learning as much as you can about life? Are you constantly experiencing new opportunities, do you read and learn, are you open to improving and stretching? You certainly score high by having chosen to read this book, but will you complete it and put into practice what you will learn here? Give yourself a mark.

4. HEALTH

How is your health? As you can see, it is holding the whole wheel together. You know it's important yet so many of us seem to take our health for granted until it lets us down. Are you looking after yourself, are you happy about your level of fitness, are you taking regular exercise? What about your diet, do you take enough rest – are you truly a 10? A 1 is clearly someone who is seriously, seriously ill, but where do you fit in on this scale? What follows over the next few chapters will assist you in improving your well-being, and much of the material we cover will impact on the quality of your health.

5. ATTITUDE

For me attitude is vital, and fittingly it comes right alongside health in holding up the wheel. What does your attitude tend to be like? Are you a positive person, constantly thinking about what you want to see happen? When something you wanted doesn't materialize, do you immediately think up a solution? Or are you a negative thinker, always worrying about what might go wrong? You are surely not a moaner – but who knows? Attitude plays a vital role in our lives, as I trust you will appreciate (especially after reading this book). Are you one of the world's great optimists – a 10 again! You can't be a 1 – they are definitely locked up.

6. CAREER

I came across a statistic which stated that 7 out of 10 people who are gainfully employed today would rather be doing something completely different. How is your career going? Does it excite you, do you love it, have you got it all marked out, do you know what you aim to achieve with it or not?

One of the great joys of doing in-house courses in companies is seeing so many people find a fresh commitment to their job – while of course others do actually resign and start a new one somewhere else. We spend a long time in our working years, so how is it for you? Is it 10 or are you nearer the 1 end, and you are actually reading this book to find the confidence to change this area in particular?

7. FINANCES

This is not about how much you have. On the MindStore course millionaires have attended as well as unemployed people. I am not asking how much you have but rather how you relate to money. Do you worry yourself sick about it, does it seem to cause stress in your life, or are you at ease with it? A 10 means you are absolutely at ease with money and you are able to go with the flow as it passes through your life. Or are you tending toward 1: so worried about money that it is absolutely limiting you?

8. SPIRITUAL LIFE

For most of the people I have met spirituality actually does exist to some degree in their lives. There are of course many who do not recognize it at all, if this is true of you, you can replace this category with something else that comes to mind. How is your spiritual life? Are you a 10: is it central to all that you do, are you committed to your practice and belief? Or are you experiencing doubt or guilt about not spending enough time on this area? Give yourself a mark for this too.

Now join up your Wheel of Life (see figure overleaf)

11

WHEEL OF LIFE

Date. . . . .

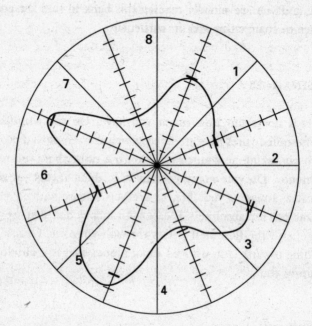

If your wheel of life looks something like this, then is it no wonder that life tends to be bumpy! The truth is that the techniques you will learn in this book will assist you in bringing balance into your life. From your wheel you should be able to see almost instantly which areas of your life might benefit most from the techniques.

I actually recommend drawing up a wheel of life every two months, so you can check your progress and see if you are spending too much time on one particular area at the expense of the others. The Wheel of Life is as a component of a major technique discussed in Chapter 9. By applying yourself to improve where necessary you can strive to be the perfect 10 at all times. Clearly if you ever reach this goal you will be an exceptional human being. However, being aware of any imbalances that can develop in our lives is a useful starting point for triggering change and growth.

I am often asked what I mean by success, and for me it is a life that is in as near perfect balance as possible. I cannot honestly say that someone who scores a 10 for career and a 4 for family is a success. It has been my experience that working to bring about this balance actually improves all the areas of the Wheel of Life.

If you have done this exercise then you will surely have real reasons for reading on and putting into practice what you will learn.

3

The Four Characteristics of Success

Inevitably I have dedicated my life to finding out what makes successful people different. I have had the joy of meeting and talking to some of Britain's most successful men and women from many walks of life. I constantly pore over their biographies, or read magazine articles devoted to them; I watch them on TV or listen to them being interviewed on radio, every chance I get. I suppose I have looked for the characteristics that the apparently gifted few have, and whether these traits can be developed in others.

My conclusion is that there are four basic elements or primary characteristics of success, and that these can be developed by anyone.

This chapter will explore the four primary characteristics that successful people have or cultivate in themselves, either intentionally or subconsciously, which enable them to be different, to stand out and achieve.

1. Put Oomph in Your Life!

From my experience people who succeed have lots of energy; they tend to rise early in the morning and go through their day absolutely focused on what they are doing, before finding a similarly high store of energy for the time they spend with their family, in their relationships or at recreation. They seem to have a zest for life and a quality of energy that allows them to embrace fully life's joys and challenges.

What is clear is that they somehow manage stress. They may create stress for themselves, always constantly moving forward overcoming setbacks, achieving, solving problems and encountering more and more, nevertheless they seem to be able to cope and cope well. Yet how many people do you and I know who seem to have opted out? Their stress gets to them, creating headaches, backaches, indigestion and other common ailments. In time, if their stress goes unmanaged, these problems can develop into more serious conditions – where I come from (Scotland) we are world leaders in heart disease, cancer and strokes.

The need to manage my own stress kicked me off on this great journey of discovery. I knew that it was undermining my happiness and affecting my self-confidence; I easily forgot things – even important information – and the stress seemed to creep up on me, directly impacting my productivity and making my health suffer. Clearly if we can manage and control stress in our lives then we can do things better, we can face new challenges which in turn can lead to more success in our careers and personal lives. In the chapters that follow you will learn to manage your personal energy so that you can live a healthier, more enjoyable life.

Indeed, this is the easiest part of the programme because all you have to do is sit back and relax – yet it may be the most important.

To my surprise I have discovered that natural talent or a special gift in a particular field don't necessarily have to be present to bring about success. I am sure we can all think of people with quite exceptional talents who have not quite made it in their field. Perhaps a lack of confidence or an unfortunate personality trait has contributed to this. And we can all think of individuals who have possessed fairly ordinary, run-of-the-mill skills who have, nevertheless, been very successful. For these people, their attitude, determination or self-confidence has won through. This phenomenon can often be seen in the fields of sport or acting. Few would make the claim that Sylvester Stallone's acting talent is one of the all-time greatest, but when you hear his story of going to hundreds and hundreds of auditions and being turned down, even laughed at, but somehow maintaining his enormous inner self-belief and desire for success, do you realize how he's got where he is today. How many with or without great talent have set out on the journey towards their dream but have given up when the going got tough? All I know is that no one gets instant success, you have to take the knocks and the falls and grow strong – usually when you are almost about to give up, success comes round the corner.

So forget about your level of talent at this point, don't let that put you off. If you have talent, then well and good – but if you don't, so what? Just read on.

2. Develop a Positive Attitude

It is my opinion that we live in a negative culture here in the UK and especially in Scotland. Everybody that I have met who has succeeded is without doubt positive. They think about what they want, they are optimistic, dynamic and are solution-oriented. On the other hand, the vast majority of people in the UK seem to think about what they *don't* want – they moan, they find excuses for why something won't or didn't work. They have a tendency to think about problems. They seem to be stuck in ruts: 'If only I had a better job/a different partner/a better car/more money.' They tend to focus on what might go wrong, they fear success as much as failure, rejection and incompetence.

Many opt out and avoid failure by doing nothing; but failure to act means they cannot learn and grow. I have never met, nor heard of, anyone who got instant success. Indeed, apparent failure leads to learning, stretching and moving on – and this is a vital clue to the secret of success. Being positive makes you overcome negative situations and move on.

I remember as a child watching the film of the life of Douglas Bader, how he overcame the loss of both legs and fought on, his tremendous self-belief and determination overwhelming – yet of course he was only human flesh and blood like you and me. Yet again the thing that stood out was his attitude, his thoughts. The other day I heard of a woman who slipped on the ice as she walked her dog; as she fell she broke her wrist. She went to hospital and, once her wrist was put right, she was back home.

This had happened over the Christmas season, and many family and friends visited and expressed their concern and sympathy for her. They tried to persuade her to come to the various parties and get-togethers they were organizing over the holidays. There was no reason why she couldn't, as long as she didn't do anything that would put undue strain on the wrist she could enjoy the festivities just as she liked. But she didn't. She continued to 'self-talk' negatively and express concern about her wrist. She moaned on and on about her wrist and turned down all invitations. She was miserable, and indeed most of her friends were almost glad in the end that she didn't come. (By 'self-talk' I mean the little conversations we have with ourselves regarding whatever is going on in our lives at any given time. This self-talk, our dominant thoughts, tend to create our reality. We are attracted subconsciously to events and activities which reinforce these thoughts, thus proving to ourselves that we are correct in what we are thinking. Clearly I am committed to developing *positive* self-talk. Think only of what you want, *not* of what you do not want.)

We have all met this paradox before: how can someone with Douglas Bader's disability go on while others limit themselves so much? The answer, yet again, is attitude.

Whatever we choose to think we choose for our lives.

Think what it might be like if you could automatically think positively. Imagine the impact on your personal and business life. Envision for a moment your family, colleagues and friends being positive. Instead of 'I can't' and 'It's impossible', what about 'I can' and 'I will'. What a cultural challenge to most of us! Read on and you'll learn how to become and remain positive.

3. Break Out of Your Limited Beliefs

Success seems to mean reaching a plateau and then reaching for a higher one. Nobody gets instant success, you need to strive, to keep pushing to new heights. We all have limiting beliefs about what we can achieve or influence. It seems to me that as children we are given a huge bag at birth, and as we grow we collect 'the luggage of life'. All our experiences, the expectations of others, all the praise and comments made in passing: all this is packed into our luggage of life.

I am sure you don't have to look far to see people who are

weighed down by their luggage, who seem to limit themselves in so many ways. To succeed we have to push on to experience new opportunities, to look beyond our current reality.

There is of course a great sense of risk about all of this. It is clearly easier to stay where and as we are, even if we are not happy with our current situation. Many have called this 'breaking out of comfort zones', others 'pushing into the adventure ground'. Frank Dick, former Director of Coaching for British Athletics, has spoken about *Mountain people* and *Valley people*. *Valley people*, he says, are stuck where it's relatively comfortable; they seek the calm and shelter of the familiar. They may talk about change but if it means hard work and moving away from what seems to be working now, then forget it. *Mountain people* take the risk of winning to test themselves on the toughest of terrains – life itself. They bounce back from bumps and bruises, they succeed, they achieve, they win.

To succeed we have to break out of our Comfort Zones and break beyond our limiting self-beliefs.

Aerodynamically a bumble bee should not be able to fly – bumble bees do not know this, and so carry on flying.

Many of us have let our self-talk limit our beliefs about our abilities and what is possible. Roger Bannister broke the four-minute mile, something that was thought to be impossible – and indeed for some 2,000 years athletes had attempted it and failed. Yet within a month of his accomplishment many others had run the mile in under four minutes; within the year over one hundred had achieved this goal. We are limited only by our thoughts and Comfort Zones. Once we break out we can set up new Comfort Zones. However, breaking out is the hard part.

The secret is we must *set goals* – this is fundamentally important, a cornerstone of success. If life is a game, then those who succeed are those who know the rules – but the vast majority of us don't even know the rules exist, let alone that the setting of goals is the most important rule of all.

The sad thing is that in all my time at school, college and university, this was never taught. I don't recall even 15 minutes of time spent on this, yet to know and understand this is in my opinion more important than all the other things I learned.

Limited beliefs and Comfort Zones will cause most people to neglect or mistrust this rule, and those people who actually do set goals also face the difficult challenge of confronting the effects of breaking out of a Comfort Zone. Others may well laugh at and ridicule them for daring to think they can achieve more or indeed change at all. Goal-setting requires no special social background, age, gender, previous experience or, as I've said before, talent; it just demands that you take the risk of succeeding and make your commitment. Others will probably resist and may even resent you setting your goals. The secret is not to tell them unless you know without doubt that they will support you. Anita Roddick of the *Body Shop* has said that 'a vision is something no one else can see', so what's the point in sharing it anyway? You just have to get on with it, the consequences of not having a vision are ageing, decay and even an early death.

I recall with amazement a senior officer of the Metropolitan Police in London telling me that most of the force is totally committed to the job. It is, he said, a complete way of life and demands dedication. He told me that the average policeman or -woman on retirement has only nine months' life expectancy unless he or she finds a new commitment or abiding interest.

I've found it interesting that, when one confronts 'Valley People' with the idea that we must have goals or we stand still and decay, that many will aggressively deny it and insist that those who do make it are either lucky or that they are cheats. Gary Player, famous as a golfer, is also famous for saying (when told by a commentator that he was a lucky golfer), 'It's funny, the more I practise the luckier I become.'

Many do not want to hear just how easy it really can be to change things; many believe it is complicated when in fact it is so easy it's almost too good to be true. Before we explain how to change, let's look at the fourth characteristic of success.

4. People Who Succeed Just Might Be Using Their Brains Differently

So far I have stated that people who do succeed manage their stress and therefore have loads of energy, they are positive and they set goals to break out of their limiting beliefs.

Limiting beliefs are like a fine mesh that seems to be right in front of our heads as we journey through life.

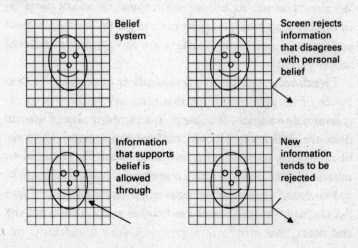

Belief system

Screen rejects information that disagrees with personal belief

Information that supports belief is allowed through

New information tends to be rejected

Our inner 'screening process' causes us to reject information that doesn't fit with our personal beliefs, and to accept only the information that coincides with our beliefs. Have you ever tried to change a person's beliefs about someone or something? If you talk about things the other person agrees with, then everything is fine – but if you talk about something the other disagrees with, then your input will probably be rejected.

The big challenge, though, is when absolutely new information comes along and therefore has no meaning to the belief system. In spite of the fact that this information is by its nature fairly non-threatening, most people will tend to reject it nevertheless. Yet where would we be today if it were not for the greats who were able to take their screens down when new information came along – who were willing to consider that the earth might be round and not flat, that we might be able to build a machine that could fly (ask the Wright Brothers!) or that polio might be cured, along with all the other wonderful breakthroughs that have been made in the past. And think of all that will surely come as we continue to progress. Where would we be if the screens were not taken down to allow humanity to grow, to develop – we must break beyond our limited beliefs. I may need you to take your screen down now.

This fourth characteristic is as important as the other three.

In 1981 two scientists, Roger Sperry and Robert Ornstein from the University of California, won the Nobel Prize for Medicine for research that had taken them 25 years. Their work led to the understanding that the two hemispheres of the neo-cortex of the brain had different characteristics or functions, that in normal usage the brain handles mental activity this way:

23

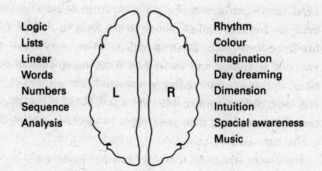

Logic
Lists
Linear
Words
Numbers
Sequence
Analysis

Rhythm
Colour
Imagination
Day dreaming
Dimension
Intuition
Spacial awareness
Music

Ornstein in particular found that people who had been specifically trained to use one hemisphere, almost to the exclusion of the other, were almost unable to use the other. He also found, however, that when the weak hemisphere was put to work in co-operation with the dominant side there was a substantial improvement in overall performance and ability.

On reflection, within the education system there has traditionally been an emphasis on the three 'Rs' – reading, 'riting and 'rithmetic – and more recently the UK Government has voiced a call for a return to these methods. Of course these are all left-brained disciplines, and are usually taught to the exclusion of any development of the right-brain faculties. All too often it has been accepted that those who excel in the academic world of the three 'Rs' were intelligent and that those who are better with their hands, who are musically or artistically talented or who are 'day-dreamers' (even this term is considered pejorative!) are less than desirable.

It may be fair to assume that as a result of this education system most of us are going around with a powerful left brain and a considerably weaker right one.

Up until Sperry's and Ornstein's research, many in the field of human potential and many self-help authors focused on the need for individuals to be positive, to look after their well-being and energy and of course to set goals so that they could break beyond their limiting beliefs. You may have found yourself motivated and excited by listening to a good motivational speaker or by reading a positive book, only to find that you soon drifted back to your old ways. What if it really is the case that people who succeed actually use their brains differently than most of us?

Inevitably, the search for an answer to this question has uncovered information about great scientists and artists. Einstein, perhaps the greatest scientist this century, actually failed mathematics at school. Clearly he must have broken out of the belief that this failure meant he was unsuited for mathematical pursuits. He is also reported to have constantly day-dreamed while at university, much to the annoyance of his professors.

The theory of relativity, one of the most significant theories of all time and one which required new physics and mathematics, was not discovered by Einstein at a desk or blackboard but rather as he lay sunbathing on a hillside. In that wonderful relaxed state he half opened his eyes to find speckled sunbeams bursting through his eyelashes. He imagined the sunbeams being large enough to sit on and, using his great sense of make-believe, he 'fired' the sunbeam back into space, deep into the universe. No matter how hard he attempted to reach into the depths of the universe he always returned back to the hillside. This fantastic creative 'right-brain' journey triggered his left brain to attempt to explain what was happening, and defying all his scientific training he used both sides of the brain to create a new scientific formula that could explain mathematically his creative breakthrough.

Many of the great artists have, as a result of similar 'dual

25

brain' usage, applied outstanding mathematical thinking in their paintings. Both brains seem to be required for exceptional results.

Ultimately, even investigations into the life of Leonardo de Vinci, perhaps the most exceptional mind ever, suggest again the necessity of using both brains to achieve outstanding performance. He excelled in mathematical and logical thinking while also being a genius with colour, rhythm and expression. Personally I have always marvelled at his fantastic imagination – to have come up with blueprints for the helicopter and submarine is impressive – however it is his perfect anatomical drawings of birds in flight that illustrate the power of his awesome imagination. Indeed, Einstein once said 'Imagination is more important than knowledge.' Without imagining bright futures and solutions to our challenges there is no future, only a grinding continuation of present reality. We need both the dreamers and the schemers.

Perhaps the most exciting thing about all of this is that, while we might assume that most of us are left-brain dominant, no matter how one-sided our brains may be (either left or right), we only need exercise the weaker part to gain proficiency with both. We need not be *either* artistic *or* scientific: we can be *both*.

I remember attending the launch of a new BBC training video by Tony Buzan, at the Institute of Directors in London back in October, 1991. Tony must be one of the greatest thinkers of our day; his countless best-selling books – published in many languages around the world – bear testament to this fact, and his MindMapping is known to many (I myself have used MindMaps for some 20 years).

At the launch Tony, with all his authority and understanding, began his presentation by saying that if this were the 1970s he could say with all confidence that we were probably using 20 per cent of the brain. If it were the 1980s he would say 10 per cent. However, he concluded, it is now the 1990s and we are using approximately a fraction of 1 per cent. In other words, we are only just scratching the surface; we are nowhere near fulfilling our potential.

The assumption I make, then, is that you are nowhere near your potential no matter how successful or how challenging your life seems to be right now. I will also assume that, due to our education system, you mainly use your left brain. Some of you will of course be fairly creative and will use the right brain more than most other people, but I firmly believe that by working to develop more of the right brain – together with managing your stress, becoming more positive, and learning to set goals – you will sense a dramatic change in how you experience life.

In Chapters 4, 5 and 6 you will learn to manage stress and create oomph in your life. You will read about the unique MindStore concept of using the right brain and will learn techniques to maintain a positive mental attitude. Chapter 7 will help you to develop an understanding of goal-setting and the possibilities for programming for success. Chapters 8 and 9 will teach you to use your intuition and to develop your fascinating right-brain faculties. Finally, in the last two chapters you will learn to make the most of sleep and how to trigger creative thought.

By the end of the book I trust you will have developed, through some interesting exercises, a way of life – a simple-to-practise process for bringing about the changes you seek for your life.

Summary

FOUR CHARACTERISTICS FOR SUCCESSFUL LIVING

1. Put *oomph* in your life. Learn to manage your stress and look after your energy levels.
2. Develop a positive attitude. Learn to think automatically about what you want at all times. Learn to become an optimistic and a solution-orientated thinker.
3. Break out of your limiting beliefs. Is your 'luggage of life' weighing you down? Learn to push out of your Comfort Zones, to stretch and experience much more of life.
4. Learn to use your brain differently. Understand the importance of using both the left- and right-brain hemispheres – learn to develop many more of the right-brain faculties of imagination, intuition and creativity.

4

Stress

How to Beat it

Stress is possibly the biggest single issue of modern life.

Yes, stress has certainly become a buzzword for the nineties. In simple terms it makes many people unable to cope with present-day life. It is the root cause of so many of today's ills: insomnia, high blood-pressure, the breakdown of relationships, heart attacks, digestive problems, sexual difficulties, arthritis, and asthma to name but a few.

No one is immune. Recent estimates suggest that in Britain some 40 million working days are lost every year at a cost of £55 million to the Department of Social Services. It affects you and me, the administrator, the teacher, the student, the banker, the bus driver, the street cleaner, the unemployed – people of all ages, either gender and any creed.

The challenge is to be able to recognize stress and of course deal with it. This can be done with anti-depressant drugs or tranquillizers, but they often exact a heavy price – illness, disease and early death. I prefer to deal with stress naturally.

Stress is a massive issue for all of us. I am sure we can all think of a person right now who suffers from its effects, and on reflection we can easily remind ourselves of our own trials with it.

The cause is simply explained by our ancestors, living in their caves and confronted by ferocious wild animals. They had a choice of running away or standing and fighting off the beasts. We know that they made their decision at a conscious level, that they thought through their options before making up their minds. At birth the human brain has some 20,000 in-built programmes – including the 'flight or fight' response we've inherited from our stone-age forebears.

This response to a threat will provide us with an instant source of energy and strength (adrenalin and noradrenalin) with which either to take flight or stand and fight. In our dim and distant past this would be experienced when facing any menacing situation; today the threat can be found in the office or even at home, in the factory or when at play. It can be found at every stage in human life, from birth through to death. It is all too clear at times of financial hardship, when we are unemployed or when we are experiencing relationship problems. It is outwardly expressed through aggression, anger, impatience, anxiety and fear.

Of course when we positively take action in fight or flight, then well and good, but when the fight or flight response is counter-productive we find it difficult to control and we suffer the harmful and even constant build-up of adrenalin until *SNAP*.

Stimulus – >Belief System – >Reaction

On my courses I use a simple model to explain the response to stress:

As we process stimuli – and these can be either external, i.e. events and situations around us, or internal, our own thoughts and attitudes – they are processed by the brain through our past experience or belief systems or, as I have

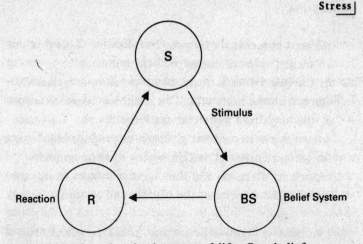

suggested before, by the luggage of life. Our belief systems will then cause a reaction to take place in our bodies.

An event has no meaning until we make sense of it through our belief systems and trigger a reaction in our bodies that will be either negative or positive depending on the status we give the event. To one person a huge queue at the supermarket check-out may be negative because he needs to catch a bus to get home in time to meet a friend. This may trigger impatience spilling over into aggression and anger. To another person of course this same queue can simply provide her with the time for some pleasurable day-dreaming.

The stress reaction, of course, diminishes as the stimulus is removed or overcome. My Stimulus – >Belief System – > Reaction model oversimplifies the truly complex response within the body, as hormones, the nervous system and other bodily functions inter-react:

1. The hypothalamus experiences a reaction of chemical nervous impulses, triggering the autonomic nervous system and resulting in changes throughout the body.
2. The stress chemicals, adrenalin and noradrenalin, are

31

released immediately into the bloodstream. This produces an instant surge of energy into the body.

3. As the blood vessels dilate, blood-pressure is increased, along with the heart rate. The breathing becomes faster as the lungs take more and shallower breaths. Cortisone within the liver converts glycogen to produce blood sugar for instant energy. The skin begins to sweat, muscle tension is increased, and the digestive system shuts down, relaxing the muscles of the bladder and rectum.

The body is highly efficient and, thank goodness, with all of the above we are able to take flight or stand and fight to survive.

The challenge we all have, though, is that the hypothalamus (which triggers the body's reaction to stress) doesn't know the difference between a real live threat such as a gunman on the rampage or an imagined one in the mind. It will trigger the response no matter what has caused our stress. Clearly the continual triggering of the hypothalamus this way is unhealthy, and over long periods leads to serious illness.

Many today find that as they become stressed they are tempted to work harder, to put in extra hours and drive further, thereby exposing themselves to more and more stress. This leads to distorted perception, causing them not to realize what is happening. The end result of course is fatigue, exhaustion or even collapse.

Perhaps the biggest challenge of all is for us to grasp that we must build in an antidote to this, indeed this has to be our absolute priority. Naturally the only way is to relax and bring down the heart rate, release muscle tension, lower blood-pressure and bring balance back to the system.

I am absolutely passionate about this. If only we could see

the sense in building relaxation breaks into the culture of every profession and business in this country we would save a fortune on health expenditure, freeing vital resources for where they are needed most. If only it were taught in every school, to make it a way of life. One simply cannot imagine the untold suffering and misery that would be avoided. The effects of stress may be the number one issue of today. The solution – relaxation – must become our primary concern.

Quality Recovery Time

If we look to sport I know from my experience of working with some of our country's most outstanding sportsmen and -women that they demand of themselves peak performance in all that they do. They know that they cannot peak in the match or the race if they have not given their all to their training and practice sessions.

From the science of sport we now know that in order to peak, to produce the very best performance, the athlete must first warm up. This makes sense of course, to loosen the muscles, to prepare before going for it. Once warmed up they will produce the performance and demand the best from themselves. Once this is done they will then 'warm down' – increasingly you will see sportsmen and -women, even whole teams go back out onto the track or field and go through a series of warm-down exercises.

Having gone through these three vital stages they will then take a complete rest or, as I call it, Quality Recovery Time (QRT). For many that may be a deep afternoon sleep or involvement in a hobby or special interest. What is clear is that QRT is vital to allow the participant to reproduce his or her best form the next day. This cycle is vital each and every day for those who are dedicated.

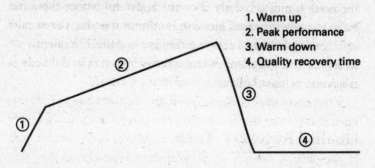

1. Warm up
2. Peak performance
3. Warm down
4. Quality recovery time

You and I are probably not athletes, however to be the person you can be, the one others around you deserve to get, you need to go through the same cycle if you are constantly to produce peak performance in your day-to-day life.

How many of us do this, though? Do you warm up before the meeting or sales pitch, before the family get-together or that important night out? Or do you just step right in and get on with it? Do you take time to warm down or do you just move on to the next hectic response? The big issue really is QRT. How can we expect to produce our best on a Friday afternoon if we have not taken time to relax earlier in the week?

The management of stress is vital; taking Quality Recovery Time is as important as turning up. But how can we reduce the build-up of stress as we journey through our day? The answer lies within us, in fact the answer lies with our thinking, our attitude.

Towards a Positive Mental Attitude

The obvious question to ask is where does the mind stop and the body begin, or where does the body end before the mind exists? Surely they melt into one another and perhaps even exist as a totality. Going back to Stimulus – >Belief System – > Reaction, it is suggested that the stress response in the body is triggered by our thinking.

The power of thought to influence the body has always fascinated me, from the simple pretence of scratching as if severely itchy in public and the effect this has on others around you, to the dramatic power of suggestion in hypnosis.

I often tell of the BBC TV programme on the work of Dr Angel Escudero, a Spanish doctor working near Valencia. The programme, part of a series on complementary medicine, illustrated the fantastic work of this great man. The scene was an operating theatre, the staff preparing for an operation. In walked a woman dressed in a hospital gown; she was not wheeled in under the influence of the pre-medication drugs and certainly no anaesthesia was administered.

The patient had a bow in her left leg that was causing arthritic complications and that needed straightening. Escudero welcomed her and settled her on the operating table. A nurse sat by her head throughout and they conversed freely with each other. Once all was in order Escudero simply asked the patient to produce liquid saliva in her mouth and to keep it there throughout. He then asked her to repeat to herself 'my leg is anaesthetized.' This was in fact her only anaesthesia.

The operation commenced, involving deep incisions into the leg, the use of clamps to hold back muscle and tissue while chisels and eventually a drill were applied to pierce right through the leg bone above and below the knee. All the time

35

the patient was fully awake, enjoying talking to her friend the nurse while Escudero and a surgical colleague got on with the task.

Once the wounds were closed and stitched around the metal rods that had been inserted through the leg, the patient simply got up and hobbled out unaided, thanking the medical staff.

This was truly amazing, and the programme showed other operations and cited evidence of some 900 being carried out this way, not only without anaesthesia but without the use of antibiotics either.

In being interviewed to explain how such events could occur without causing the patient severe pain and indeed shock, Escudero replied that the secret was that 'the human mind is simple.' If the mouth contained saliva then the brain would process that to mean that the patient was indeed relaxed and certainly not in a state of panic. Further, by stating that the leg was anaesthetized and insensitive then it had to be so. The interviewer was obviously challenged by this straightforward explanation and the programme continued with further proof of the many applications of this 'secret' that Escudero had discovered.

The power of mind over body in this case almost takes Stimulus – >Belief System – >Reaction to the extreme, but if it has such meaning then what happens when someone constantly self-talks into failure, unhappiness, illness and all the other obvious negative experiences?

I have had great fun using muscle-testing with sports teams to demonstrate dramatically how thoughts impact the body. Muscle testing is drawn from Kinesiology, a fascinating diagnostic tool used by many complementary medical practitioners. (Might I suggest you read *Your Body Doesn't Lie* by Dr John Diamond?)

I do this by testing the strength in an arm, asking the person to hold it out full length to one side, at shoulder height, and to make a fist. Facing the person I place one hand on his or her weaker shoulder and the other on the outstretched fist; I then push down on the outstretched arm while the person does all he or she can to resist. This will give an indication of the person's strength.

If I then ask the person to hold a cigarette in the mouth (having given him or her time to rest) and repeat the muscle-testing pressure, the person finds that all strength is gone and that he or she cannot resist at all. Many other challenging substances can be tested similarly. I will then go on to test the person's strength while I repeat positive and negative words such as 'winning' and 'losing' or 'love' and 'hate'.

It may seem silly, however under the influence of the positive words people are generally even stronger than normal, while the negative words seem to sap their energy.

On first seeing this many people attempt to dismiss the results as a hoax or a trick on my part, often trying to suggest that I have changed position or that I am using different pressure. The truth is that my intention is to use the same amount of effort each time. In his book John Diamond provides photographs and results of more objective methods, which use machines for measuring the resistance.

All this fascinates me and of course many of my audience, but the point is that the words and thoughts we use will affect our bodies and of course our outcomes.

I have taught the MindStore programme extensively across Britain from the shop floor to the boardroom, to people from all walks of life. It has been my experience that there is one constant underlying force that is ever-present regardless of status, background or situation. For me this force explains human existence and all its limitations of hopelessness and out-standing successes: a person's attitude or, to put it another way, the quality of the inner voice.

Once again for me this is one of the biggest issues we face in modern life. I believe the great tendency in our culture here in the UK is, for the most part, to be negative. The inner voice is self-critical, limiting and is often in the 'I can't' mode, holding most people back. The task before us is to silence the negative and the 'I can't' and to build the 'I can.'

We must develop positive self-talk and learn to believe in it, then we can all move forward.

To my absolute joy the newscaster Martin Lewis was quoted late in 1993 as saying that the news is far too negative. I can only agree. We are a nation of news-hounds. It is very rarely positive and when it is it is usually relegated to a minor spot at the end of the broadcast or to precious few column inches. There is so much good going on, fantastic achievements in every town, city and region of this country, but we don't hear about or focus on it – instead, every night you can hear of famine, war, violence and crime.

Now, before you react and say that we cannot ignore these great challenges, I am in total agreement. All I ask is that we focus our reporting and observing on solutions and possibili-ties. If we continue to look only at the problems then we will surely only find more of them; clearly if we focus on solutions then they will also have to appear.

There are so many examples one could use. One of my great joys is to work with leading sportsmen and -women – Liz McColgan has to be one of the greatest. Indeed many who know about these things believe that she may be the greatest athlete of all time. I remember the report from a London broad-sheet the day of her 10,000 metres world championship race in Tokyo. Liz knows all about the importance of being positive. The report that morning was from a press conference the night before, when some of the key contenders for the 10,000-metre title were interviewed.

One of the journalists asked a competitor, 'If you don't win, who do you think will?' The runner answered. This then led to others asking their country's representative who they thought would win if they themselves didn't. McColgan was last to be asked, and while all the rest had named competitors, she answered 'Look, I've told you before, I am the only one who is going to win.' I loved it! This to me is what it is all about. We can never give an ounce to the negative. Liz was there for only one thing. Total concentration and commitment are vital. As you know, Liz did indeed win the gold medal, in unbelievable conditions. I am sure you can remember the commentary from TV presenters that night – what a joy.

From a totally different world comes the story of the remarkable Victor Frankel, the world-famous psychiatrist who spent three years of his life as a prisoner in the horrifying concentration camps of Dachau and Auschwitz. In his book *Man's Search for Meaning* he describes the suffering and degradation suffered at the hands of the Nazis. He witnessed friends and relatives being crammed into graves to be buried alive or being thrown into the gas chambers. This kind of personal day-to-day trauma is, thank goodness, beyond most people's imagination. He highlights throughout the book that those who survived shared a common yet essential ingredient: attitude. He states, 'Everything can be taken from a man but one thing: the last of human freedoms – to choose one's attitude in any given set of circumstances, to choose one's own way.'

I could fill this book with anecdotes of the great and accomplished, and I know it is their attitude that made all the

39

difference. Yet we continue to be a nation of moaners. Generally the positive few are scorned and laughed at; some misinterpret their positive attitude as something that's somehow improper. Others misread it as 'showing off' or gaining good fortune at the expense of others' misfortune.

To be positive often runs against the prevailing tide. It's socially acceptable to moan even our simplest greetings: 'How are you?' will at best be answered with 'Not too bad, thanks.'

I will never forget arriving at the offices of a major British company to do a presentation for the manager. It was early in the morning, a day in early June with the sun high in the sky; the birds were singing and it was a joy to be alive. The reception area of the office was situated in a rather spacious hallway. I was asked to wait a few minutes until the manager was available. I stood focused in one corner, patiently waiting, when a door opened about 30 feet away.

The man who entered greeted me with 'What a wonderful day.' He was full of the joys of life and in tremendous spirits. Incidentally, this wasn't the boss – this man walked over to the reception desk and addressed one of the administrators there, 'I don't suppose, Helen,' he said, 'that my return is back yet from head office?' This return was clearly important to him – he was a salesman who was paid only by results, his income depended on it. When she replied 'No' he immediately used a common expletive and his posture changed in an instant from being upright and alert with joy and zest to being slouched with little or no life. He turned and dragged himself back towards the door. In seconds he had gone from someone who could have achieved anything, someone who had the vitality to do so, to a drained, lifeless wreck.

The great truth is that the post had not arrived yet and the fax machine was still to be cleared from overnight, not to mention that the telephone exchange was busy and any one of the incoming calls could have been for him. The tragedy is he didn't realize how much his irresponsible reaction affected the rest of his day, not to mention the effect on all of his colleagues, who now observed him returning back through the door and who may well have contributed to his scathing complaints about head office and the administration workers there.

As I see it we have a choice, and I can only agree with Victor Frankel. Each of us rises into our day with our energy restored from a good night's sleep – as long as we are eating and sleeping well then we will have all the energy we need for the day ahead. Half of us throw the better part of that energy away in the way we wake up and greet the morning: usually the alarm goes off – itself a stressor – followed by 'Oh no, it's Monday!'

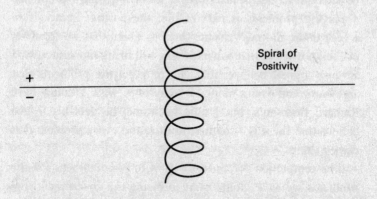

Spiral of
Positivity

+
–

We have the choice to rise up what I call the spiral of positivity, looking on the bright side – or, as is all too normal, to begin the slide down the spiral of negativity. You will find by observing your own thoughts or by listening to others' conversations that one negative thought or word will immediately lead to another.

To be positive means to push against the prevailing tide. When I first started in this field very few people were interested and of course many were cynical and would laugh and attempt to put it all down as phoney American nonsense. When you start to use it in your life you may encounter negative reactions at first, but fairly quickly those around you will notice the change in you. They may even begin to enjoy it since you will be a better person to be with. Certainly you will have more energy and be much more fun.

The truth is that to be alive is to have problems. Who can honestly say that they don't have any? I used to think that to be successful was to live a life without problems; at some level in my mind an image of a beautiful sun-drenched beach and a life of luxury was ever-present. The simple reality is that to be successful means just solving more and more problems.

Having problems is part of life; the positive stance is to accept them, indeed welcome them as a sign that we are alive, in the knowledge that solving them will bring more success. I am also a great believer that you only get the problems that are yours and yours alone. I sometimes wish I could have Richard Branson's, but I only get mine, he gets his. I also believe that there is a solution to each and every problem that comes along.

The temptation for most of us is to blame others for the problems we have. Some want to blame the government, the unions, the bosses; it's my mother's fault; my father's; it's the way I was brought up. It's all too easy to do this, and next time you point the finger of blame at someone else, realize that three fingers point right back to you while your thumb points to heaven.

Take ownership, take control and claim your problems as your own – then resolve to solve them.

Napoleon Hill, who wrote the great *Think and Grow Rich* and, with W. C. Stone, *Success through a Positive Mental Attitude*, said that 'At times of adversity there is a seed of equal or greater benefit.' There is always good that can come from a situation; your task when faced with even the most trying time is to look for the opportunity, the potential within it and focus on that.

Many of us, the positive thinkers, prefer not to use the word 'problem' at all since the word itself implies difficulty, being stuck in some unpleasant situation. We prefer to use the word *challenge*; this has obvious positive connotations and its use brings an immediate sense of confidence that a solution is on the way.

Once you decide to become positive, even in the face of adversity, the secret is to stick with it. Self-talk yourself into believing that a solution is imminent and that the difficulty will soon be gone. When times have been tough for me (and they have been, I can assure you) I have found myself repeating mentally, 'This will pass, I know the tide will turn.' I have also found great strength by stepping back from an apparently big challenge to give myself time. I will go back to it a day later, usually after having allowed my subconscious mind to get on with looking for solutions, only to find that the situation no longer seems so threatening.

This positive approach has allowed me to change my inner focus. When I used to think about a problem all day long I just kept seeing it in all its strength. Once I changed my thinking to be more solution-orientated I started automatically to find them. It is really quite simple and you will find that your attitude will attract people, places and opportunities that reinforce your expectations. When you first begin to choose the positive it may well amaze you how quickly opportunities for moving forward seem to appear, as if from nowhere, how people almost by coincidence come to you to assist – it can be quite exciting.

Let's be realistic. You and I are alive and therefore we face the challenges of being alive, we cannot escape the way life is. In life we will come across bereavement, we will suffer loss, illness, we can have accidents, face redundancy, rejection, disappointment and so on. This is it, this is the way it is, while everything around you seems to be going wrong then you must be aware that you have absolute control of your response to it.

You can choose your attitude. In deciding to be positive you will decide to be strong. You will not be fazed by the situation and this will be a source of encouragement not only to yourself but to those around you. You will more than likely see a way out. This constant response will dramatically improve your chances of success. Please note that this can only be developed by working at it all day and every day. HOW CAN YOU BE POSITIVE WITH THE BIG CHALLENGES OF LIFE IF YOU ARE NOT WITH THE LITTLE ONES?

Mind Your Language

This means we have got to get to fundamentals. Your thoughts and your speech will reflect your attitude. Your choice of words will indicate just how you think. If you want to change from being negative to being positive, then the starting point is to change your language – choose to use only positive words. Stop the negative day-to-day language you use. Listen to the words you use and you will find that many of them have a negative meaning. That they lead you in a direction you surely do not want to go.

I once heard a simple definition: positive thinking is thinking about what you want, negative thinking is thinking about what you don't want.

It is worth while taking a sheet of paper and listing the negative words you tend to use in your vocabulary, then finding a positive replacement for each one.

Negative	Positive
• Problem	• Challenge
• I forget	• I will remember shortly
• It's freezing	• It could be warmer
• I'm feeling sick	• I could be feeling better
• I'm tired	• I could have more energy

On the MindStore course I suggest that if we consider the brain to be a kind of bio-computer, then the words and thoughts we have and use will serve as programmes to the brain. If we go back to Stimulus – >Belief System – >Reaction, then we must be careful to ensure the response we want by using the positive alternative to the negative tendency in our language.

In the computer world the term GIGO is used – it means Garbage In, Garbage Out. It makes sense: if the wrong information is fed into the computer, then the wrong information will come out. Of course if good is fed in, then good will come out.

Delete that Programme

You will find that you need to work at changing your language, and using a trigger will help greatly. I recommend to everyone that they use the following phrase:

'Delete that Programme.'

With its computing associations it will work on the bio-computer – your brain:

Get into the practice of saying this to yourself immediately you hear yourself using negative words or thinking negative thoughts. Then use this to prompt you to replace the negative word with a positive alternative. For example 'I think we have a problem' – Delete that Programme – 'I think we have a challenge to face here;' 'I feel quite ill' – Delete that Programme – 'I could feel a lot better just now.'

Commit yourself to this and you will soon notice the negativity not only in yourself but in those around you. You will also notice how positive language affects the results you achieve in your day-to-day business.

Work at this, it will amaze you just how negative your language tends to be – and it will astound you how quickly you can change to the positive with this tool. Using positive language will quickly affect your attitude and therefore your enjoyment of life and even your energy and well-being. As I always say, *'It Only Works.'*

Positive Affirmations

Another great tool is to put together a number of positive affirmations or statements that you repeat to yourself at various times of the day. They will assist your development of positive self-talk and can often have an immediate impact on your behaviour and the outcomes you achieve.

There are many popular affirmations; perhaps the most

famous is the one developed by Emile Coue, a French pharmacist who found that by giving his patients an instruction to repeat along with their medicine, they seemed to recover quickly. His famous affirmation is *'Every day and in every way I am getting better and better.'* To this many have added 'stronger and stronger' or 'happier and happier'; feel free to make your own changes to this basic affirmation.

By simply repeating the affirmation, together with maintaining an attitude of belief and enthusiasm, people do report improvement. Affirmations are written in a special way so that they can impact the subconscious and therefore bring about the desired state of being. They are made up of the three 'Ps': they are *positive*, *present tense* and *personal*. I recommend starting with the word 'I' or 'my' and ending with the word 'now'. That takes care of two Ps, while the other is the positive middle – for example:

'I am a total winner and I am completely successful at everything I undertake to do now.'

or

'My financial matters are in perfect order now.'

The Canadian Brian Tracey, who has developed very good personal development training courses, recommends rising each morning with, 'I believe something wonderful is going to happen today' – he suggests saying this five times before going into your day – he also enthuses about affirming to yourself five times 'I like myself.' And there's always 'I feel happy, I feel healthy, I feel terrific!'

It is easy to dismiss these simple approaches to creating change, but have a go for 10 days, using your own personal affirmation, and see what happens.

As you might expect I am an absolute enthusiast. I remember a time when my finances were, to say the least, challenged. I

was in considerable difficulty with a huge overdraft and little
funds to pay necessary expenses. I came across a fantastic
approach to dealing with this type of situation; together with
my positive enthusiasm I was able to turn the thing around. I
kept on repeating to myself whenever my financial worries
came to my head, 'My personal and business finances are in
perfect order now.' I took my cheque book and wrote on each
cheque, in bold black pen:

With joy and pleasure	Date _____
I Pay	
	£
	Signature

and on the reverse side of my cheques:

This amount goes out into the world and enriches it before coming back to me multiplied

You can imagine the effect of this on the staff [...] They all found it hilarious, and when I visited to ca[...] business there they all kind of stared at me in disbel[...] me a curious thrill to realize that they all thought I ...as nuts; more important, it worked! My confident affirmations had a huge impact on my self-belief and therefore the attitude of those with whom I was doing business. I can honestly say that my income has indeed multiplied and that I am now free of financial worries, and have been since the moment I adopted these positive affirmations.

If you are interested in finding out more about this, get a hold of books such as *The Richest Man in Babylon* by George S. Clason, Mark Fisher's excellent *The Instant Millionaire* or, my favourite, *Moneylove* by Jerry Gillies.

I receive many letters from MindStore members who, having done the course, put the techniques into use. Recently Tessa, the Managing Director of a marketing and public relations company, wrote to me to say:

Having attended the MindStore course in Glasgow earlier this year and having found it a great inspiration and motivating force for my business, I discovered in July that I had cancer and would have to have a kidney removed.

Using the MindStore techniques, with the backup support of the tapes, I overcame the challenge of my illness, returning to work – on a part-time – seven days after the operation, and functioning fully within a few weeks.

My consultant was amazed by the speed of my recovery and the fact that I appeared to overcome any discomfort and side-effects which he predicted I would encounter. Whenever he presented me with the probable side-effects I 'deleted that programme'.

Three months later, with my health fully restored, my posi-

tive energy is once again concentrated on the other aspects of my life.

I know that Tessa is glad to share her story with others, as it will encourage many who read it to start using the techniques.

Believe me, *'It Only Works!'* – keep an eye and ear on your thinking and develop self-talk to support your aspirations.

AFFIRMATIONS

- Every day and in every way I am getting better and better.
- I am in perfect health now.
- I am living a happy, healthy and prosperous life now.
- Perfect health and abundant energy are mine now.
- Perfect health, financial security and unconditional love are mine now.
- I am healthy, wealthy and wise now.
- The food I am about to eat is tasty, nourishing and enjoyable.
- My financial matters are in perfect order now.
- I have all the time I need for my life now.
- I am always in the right place at the right time to meet the right people now.
- Laughter ripples through every cell of my body now.
- I enjoy and appreciate everyone I meet. I like them and they like me.
- I am a total winner and I am completely successful at everything I undertake to do now.
- I free myself from the burden of blaming others and take full responsibility for my life now.
- Everything that happens is for a reason and serves me now.

- I have perfect elimination, mentally, emotionally and physically now.
- I manifest abundance in my life now and always.
- I know all my needs are perfectly met at all times.
- I am a rich human being abounding with potential now.
- I give and receive freely now.

The Glass Screen

Another technique that can reinforce your positivity and maintain your energy comes from the world of sport. When I started to get involved with leading sportsmen and -women I began researching as much as I could about their techniques for developing the positive mental attitude that seems so important to them.

I read in Seve Ballesteros' book *Natural Golf* how he imagines himself inside a bubble. He uses this image to focus all his energy on winning and getting his attitude right. He particularly highlights his use of it to heighten his concentration during his Open Championship winning campaign at Royal Lytham and St Anne's in 1979: 'It was like a pane of glass.' That is, he was enclosed with his thoughts – nothing negative could get in.

If we go back to another Spaniard, Angel Escudero and his explanation of the simplicity of the human brain, then you might appreciate why I am such an enthusiast for pretending I am in a bell jar or a bubble or even a jam jar. The moment I sense the negative attitude of people around me I immediately imagine the tune from the TV programme *Thunderbirds*, and with it an imaginary glass screen falls around me to protect me just like a gigantic jam jar. I tell myself that the screen of glass will resist negativity but will allow positivity to flow through. This means I can continue to converse and stay involved with those around me, but that I won't be affected by their negativity. I remain strong and positive while maintaining my confidence and self-belief. Again, *'It Only Works!'* – why not try it for yourself?

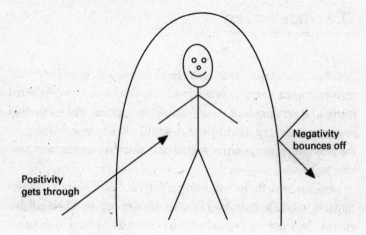

Positivity gets through

Negativity bounces off

All of these little techniques when used day to day will give you the edge. Recently I had to speak at two company sales conferences in England. They were both at big venues with around 1500 people each. As I arrived the day before in each case to check the arrangements, others who were on the programme were doing rehearsals with the autocue and checking their slides and timing. There were lots of people who were nervous and, as you might expect, excited about the prospect of the conferences.

In these sorts of situations I am able to remain calm by self-talking, especially when any doubt sneaks in. I 'delete that programme' and tell myself 'My delivery will be excellent and I will run to time. Inside my head I have all the experience and capability to produce the finest possible speech for my clients and I will.' Yet again, *'It Only Works.'*

I can only state that I can produce absolutely amazing levels of personal energy for hours and hours simply by putting all of this to work for me, and so can you – positivity and oomph go hand in hand.

Summary

1. Stimulus – >Belief System – >Reaction. Understand the importance of this simple model. Learn to control the quality of the input through your thoughts so as to ensure that you *choose* your response to life rather than just automatically react to it.
2. Introduce Quality Recovery Time to your daily schedule.
3. Use DELETE THAT PROGRAMME and replace your negative language with positive alternatives.
4. Positive affirmations make for positive results!
5. Learn from Seve Ballesteros and use an imaginary screen to protect yourself from the negativity of others.

Relaxation Techniques

The House on the Right Bank

Returning to the link between attitude and stress management, we now know the importance of relaxation: we need to take Quality Recovery Time. I believe it has to become a way of life. Built into every day must be key sessions of 5, 10 or 15 minutes of deep relaxation in order to dissipate any build-up of stress while replenishing our energy levels so that we can journey on.

Relaxation is the natural response to stress, and once learned it is easy to use. It brings with it many outstanding extra benefits.

I've mentioned Tony Buzan and his 1991 video launch at the Institute of Directors. He stated that to be totally creative, to be at our very best we must learn to use both brains as

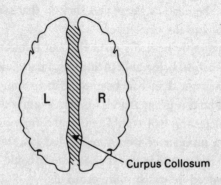

Curpus Collosum

though we could stand on the corpus collosum of the brain and reach into both sides of the neo-cortex at will.

We know that the way to trigger right-brain thinking, i.e. imaginative, intuitive, creative thought, is by relaxing.

Think about it – have you ever noticed how you tend to get great ideas when you are away from your work-place, on holiday, walking the dog, having a bath or even lying in your bed or sitting by the fireside?

There is a wonderful story about Thomas Edison, who once noted that his best ideas came to him when he was lying in bed, especially in the middle of the night – away from his desk or workbench when he was relaxed, even drowsy and ready for sleep. He said that it dawned on him that if he could re-create that special state of mind when he was at his work he could solve more problems and of course become more successful.

One night while sitting by his fireside at home with a friend he noticed after a while how he was nice and relaxed, even drowsy. It occurred to him that this was similar to how he felt when he came up with his great ideas or flashes of insight. He thought that he could train himself to capture the creative moment by sitting in front of the fire until he became drowsy, just at the edge of sleep, and then in that state somehow find solutions to his challenges.

Apparently he had a go at this but found that he would fall asleep before being able to address a particular issue. Later he used a large steel ball bearing to help him stay awake – he would hold it in one hand, his arm slightly outstretched. If he fell asleep the ball would fall to the floor and wake him up. Over a number of weeks he trained his brain to stay on the edge of sleep, and in this special state he could focus his thinking and indeed be much more creative.

What Edison didn't know then was that by being so relaxed he was actually bringing the right-brain faculties into play. As he learned to re-create this state of mind at will, he went on to bring his expanded faculties to good use when and where he needed them.

You will have noticed that at night you are far more creative in your dreams than in your thoughts during the day. Perhaps one way to look at this is: during the day the left brain tends to be dominant and during the night the right brain tends to be dominant.

By learning to relax and use the right brain at will anywhere you will trigger greater use of your thinking capacity. I have also discovered that the same state of mind can be used to bring rapid change in performance and personal growth in all areas of life. You will learn how to use this state in many ways as you continue to read through the rest of this book.

If you learn to relax, your stress will dissipate and your right brain will benefit, too. By learning to use the MindStore relaxation exercises and practising them you will certainly be able to produce an outstanding Quality Recovery Time in a matter of seconds anywhere and at any time. Making the MindStore relaxation a way of life will bring you benefits and improvements in your day-to-day existence.

The First Stage of the MindStore Technique

All the MindStore methods involve a relaxed state and, as you will find out in later exercises, this easy-to-use concept will greatly assist you in developing right-brain activities that bring results in day-to-day situations.

Read through the relaxation exercise that follows and then find a comfortable position, preferably in a quiet room, and practise it on your own. You may feel that reading it out loud and recording it for play-back will assist you, or if you wish have a friend read it to you. The ellipses (...) indicate where you should pause as you read it through out loud.

You will find that you can do this relaxation exercise lying down or sitting in a chair. I prefer to have beginners learn while sitting, as my thinking is that if you can master this while sitting then you will probably be able to do it anywhere – on a plane, on a coach or train, in a dressing room, at your desk. I tell you I can do it anywhere – even while standing on the tube at rush hour in London.

You will want a straight-backed position with both feet firmly on the floor and your hands resting on your lap, palms down. Be sure to have nothing on your lap or anything in your hands, you may even wish to remove your glasses if you wear them (and removing contact lenses for the first exercise can make a big difference).

EXERCISE 1 – A SIMPLE RELAXATION
Close your eyes and begin breathing in a regular and slow manner. We will now begin to focus your mind and body on relaxing into a healthy state of being. As I mention different parts of your body, concentrate on each one and focus your thinking on producing relax-ation.

[Concentrate on your scalp... Repeat mentally after me:]

I feel my scalp...I am aware of my scalp...my scalp is

relaxing...I feel my scalp relax...my scalp is very relaxed... My forehead is relaxing...I feel my forehead relax...my forehead is very relaxed... Now my eyelids begin to relax...I can feel then become limp, almost heavy...my eyelids are relaxed... This relaxation is now spreading around my eyes and beginning to relax the muscles of my face... I feel my face relax – very, very relaxed now... My mouth is relaxed...I feel my mouth relax...my tongue...and now my throat begins to relax...I feel my throat relax... My head is completely relaxed, as my neck now feels the pleasant experience of relaxation flow slowly downwards to my shoulders...

My shoulders are becoming very relaxed...this warm feeling is getting deeper and deeper, my shoulders are very, very relaxed... This deep relaxation is now flowing into my arms...my arms are becoming very limp as the upper muscles of my arms now relax...all the muscles of my arms are becoming limp and deeply relaxed, right down to my fingertips...

My chest and upper back are now relaxing...a warm glow of deep relaxation completely relaxes my chest...my chest is very, very relaxed... This healthy relaxing glow continues to flow down into my abdomen and lower back... The muscles of my stomach are very relaxed, very, very relaxed indeed... My pelvic region now relaxes as the warm sensation continues to flow downwards as I become more and more relaxed...

The relaxation now flows into my thighs...the powerful muscles of my thighs are now completely relaxed...right to the bones... I am so relaxed just like the rest of my upper body...it flows further into my knees...my knees are now very, very relaxed... The relaxation is now spreading into my calves, becoming ever more relaxed, very, very relaxed, and on down to my ankles... They are now relaxed, so relaxed...and now to my feet...my toes...the soles of my feet and heels...completely, completely relaxed... I enjoy the wonderful benefits of complete relaxation now...

When ready I am going to count from one to seven to gradually readjust to come out of this healthy state of deep relaxation... 1...2...3...4...now beyond the midpoint, when I open my eyes I will be wide awake and revitalized both physically and mentally...5, I begin to adjust my body...6, I prepare to open my eyes...and 7, I open my eyes and am wide awake now, both physically and mentally alert.

It may seem on first reading the relaxation that it will take a long time to do. You will be surprised just how you feel about time once you've done it. Over a short period, even just a few practice sessions, you will be able to dispense with the above and achieve the same relaxation very quickly on your own.

I use this approach and the rest of the techniques that follow to focus my mind completely in a matter of seconds or over a longer time – say 10 or 15 minutes depending on my situation and need. I practise this relaxation technique three times a day and it makes a wonderful difference.

Stage 2: The Introduction of Imagination

Let's remind ourselves that relaxation will assist you to dissipate your physical stress and give you access to much more of your thinking capacity by accessing your right-brain faculties.

At a simple level, the first exercise will help with physical relaxation, but you probably will have noticed that your mind does not rest, it just keeps on thinking, even distracting you from the task of concentrating on each part of your body. This is normal and we all face this challenge, however it is best that we work at bringing it under control.

Going back to an earlier point about where the body begins and the mind ends and our understanding that every thought must be processed (the Stimulus – >Belief System – >Reaction response), it is important to relax not only the body but also the mind. Many forms of meditation can totally relax the mind by making it focus on one thought, such as the flutter of a candle or the constant repetition of a mantra. We can also direct the mind to think about relaxing scenes such as a beach or a warm hillside. If we are thinking about a relaxing scene and we truly engage in it by focusing on what it looks like, smells like, feels like and even tastes like, then our brain will think we are actually there and become even more relaxed.

My aim with the MindStore technique is to teach you to relax both physically and mentally. This will take care of stress and of course trigger right-brain activity. Then, through the process, to focus the right brain and your expanded thinking on dynamically solving your problems, improving your performance and bringing any changes you desire into your life.

I make some assumptions – for example, in the relaxed state we can begin to reach into the right-brain faculties, but the left brain will remain dominant. My idea was to develop a process that would involve the logic of the left brain while directly developing the strength of the right.

Imagination is an outstanding part of the right brain. Remember what Einstein said: 'Imagination is more important than knowledge.' He realized that if we use only the knowledge we have today we will produce no growth or fantastic future breakthroughs in any area of life. Think about it, there is nothing around you right now that first of all wasn't an imagined thought in someone's brain. Go on, look around you. Right now I am sitting at a huge table in my study: someone imagined the particular design and the staining of the wood. Beside me now there is that modern necessity, the fax machine – can you imagine the extent of imagined possibilities that was necessary before one of these was invented? What about the propelling pencil that I am writing with?

The truth is, nothing exists without the spark of imagination in the right brain, which is then picked up by the left, which will then think out how it can be made reality.

So I wanted to use imagination, and if I could structure it to pretend we were journeying further into the right brain then surely I would be onto a winner. I went through many phases before finally settling for the programme I now teach on the MindStore courses.

Once you are physically relaxed, I call this state Physical Foundation, a state in which we can access – or, if you like, build on – the right side of the brain. I have also found that taking a few seconds to imagine being somewhere relaxing assists this process and allows my creative faculties to prepare themselves for what follows. The more I went through this ritual or pattern of behaviour, the more I seemed to understand at a deeper level what I wanted to achieve within my brain. It seemed to set up expectations of improved outcomes or performance.

Once physically and mentally relaxed you have reached the state of Physical and Mental Foundation, or simply Foundation. You might imagine being in a state where you are standing on the corpus collosum between both hemispheres of the brain, a point at which you could freely access both the left and right brain at once.

To develop the right hemisphere and to provide a vehicle of access I decided to engage the imagination fully but in a controlled manner. Once at Foundation we will imagine a river bank; you will pretend that you are standing on the bank of a river. The river will be behind you and you will be facing an imagined landscape. You will create or imagine the landscape – you can choose to remember a beautiful landscape from your travels or envision a totally imagined one.

We will call this landscape the right bank of the river. Now it is not on your right-hand side, remember the landscape is in front of you and the river behind you. We will call this the right bank to associate it with the right brain, and since we will be using the faculty of imagination it would seem to be an appropriate way to access the right hemisphere.

To assist you, you will then imagine standing on lush green grass, you will feel your feet on the ground. Overhead the sky is blue and the air is warm and fresh with the scent of a meadow. Fully engage all your senses in pretending you are there. The landscape stretches out before you. I do not want to limit your imagination but you can have friendly animals, wonderful flowers, trees, hills and even snow-capped mountains in the distance – it is all up to you.

You may find that you could make your initial attempts better, you may feel that you could be more creative, but as you might expect it will get better the more you do it. You

63

can even change the landscape as you become more proficient, however I suspect you will eventually settle on one landscape and that will serve the purpose.

The idea now is to walk into the landscape, focusing your imagination as you go to create specific features of the land around you. As you continue to walk into the scene before you, you will be intent on finding a special location. An ideal place where you will build in your imagination a house, a very special house, a large house, a house of your choice. We will call it 'The House on the Right Bank'.

This imagined house will provide you with the structure for developing all the wonderful tools that will impact so many areas of your life. I have taught this to thousands and thousands of people all over the country and, as you might expect, the range of houses and designs would do the world's architects proud.

Clearly the house is up to you, it's your creation. The only limitation I place on you is that the roof must be red in colour. If it helps, get yourself a copy of a magazine like *Country Life*; in it you will find many wonderful examples of potential Houses on the Right Bank. Perhaps you will want to use a house you remember from some holiday or travel experience. You could incorporate a number of buildings into some fantastic combination or you could come up with a futuristic structure or a scene from science fiction. It really is up to you.

Inside this house we will develop a number of rooms that you will learn to use for focusing your thinking, where you will develop the power of your own mind. There will be a room that you will use to manage your stress and produce instant energy. This room can be used to take away the physical manifestations of stress such as a headache. There will be a room in which you will learn to sleep better, to improve your

64

creativity and to solve problems. Another room will be the place where you learn to set goals, a room that will cause you to break out of your own limiting beliefs. Finally you will develop your own rooms as the concept and your results will open up your own imagination and get your own ideas flowing.

At this point it may seem a bit adventurous, after all most of us tend not to be creative and actually most have some degree of difficulty in using our imagination. You may wish to recall your childhood and just how fantastic your make-believe was back then.

The good news is that, with just a little practice, you will get better and better at imagining your house. *It only works.*

Incidentally, can you imagine the fun children have with this? The MindStore Discovery courses for children have a wonderful impact on them. The houses they come up with are truly amazing. Children take to the techniques like ducks to water and the results they produce in their lives are a joy to behold.

OK – when you are ready go through the second exercise (below) and build the outer construction of your House on the Right Bank. We will go inside and create the rooms in later exercises. Once again you will find that you gain best results by recording the exercise and playing it back to yourself, or by having a friend read it to you. You can of course simply memorize as much as you can if you prefer. Whatever you do you will be doing just fine.

EXERCISE 2 – THE HOUSE ON THE RIGHT BANK
Once again find a comfortable position in your chair, close your eyes and begin breathing in a regular and slow manner. We will now begin to focus your mind and body on relaxing into a healthy state of being.

Again, as I mention each part of your body concentrate on it and focus your thinking on producing relaxation.

Take a deep breath and relax...take another deep breath and relax...take a deep breath and relax... My scalp is relaxed, I feel my scalp relaxed... My forehead is relaxed, I feel my forehead relaxed... My eyelids are relaxed, I feel my eyelids relaxed... My face is relaxed, I feel my face relaxed... My tongue is relaxed, I feel my tongue relaxed... My jaw is relaxed, I feel my jaw relaxed... My throat is relaxed, I feel my throat relaxed...

My shoulders are relaxed, I feel my shoulders relaxed... My arms and hands are relaxed, I feel my arms and hands relaxed... My upper back is relaxed, I feel my upper back relaxed... My chest is relaxed, I feel my chest relaxed... My lower back is relaxed, I feel my lower back relaxed...

My abdomen is relaxed, I feel my abdomen relaxed... My hips are relaxed, I feel my hips relaxed... My thighs are relaxed, I feel my thighs relaxed... My knees are relaxed, I feel my knees relaxed... My calves are relaxed, I feel my calves relaxed... My ankles are relaxed, I feel my ankles relaxed... My toes are relaxed, I feel my toes relaxed... My soles are relaxed, I feel my soles relaxed... My heels are relaxed, I feel my heels relaxed...

Take a deep breath and relax... I will now imagine that

I am in a very special place of relaxation... I fully pretend that I am there... I can see the scene all around me...I can smell the scent in the air and I can hear all the wonderful sounds... I will give myself a short period to fully enjoy this [20 to 30 seconds approx.].

Once again I take a deep breath and relax... I will now adjust and imagine that I am standing on a river bank...the river is behind me and I am facing a wonderful landscape...

I can feel my feet on the lush green grass...overhead the sky is blue and the air is fresh with the scent of the meadow...I can hear the sounds of this wonderful land before me...

I will shortly walk into the landscape, creating its scenery as I go in order to find the ideal location for my house...

I now begin this beautiful journey, giving myself some time to create the landscape all around me [1 minute approx.]

I now focus my mind on the site where I will construct my House on the Right Bank... First I create the walls, their height and features are as I choose... Now the windows...the roof is red... The entrance is welcoming and attractive to me... I have now created the outer construction of my House on the Right Bank... I will use it to achieve whatever I desire for my life...

I now leave the house and return to the river's edge... I feel the lush green grass beneath my feet. I will shortly count from 1 to 7 and gradually adjust to come out of this healthy state of deep relaxation...

1...2...3...4...now beyond the midpoint, when I open my eyes I will be wide awake and revitalized both physically and mentally...5, I begin to adjust my body...6, I prepare to open my eyes...and 7, I open my eyes and am wide awake now, both physically and mentally alert.

Again I trust you enjoyed it; please bear in mind that you will improve on it each time you continue to practise. I have already mentioned the use of affirmations, those positive statements in the present tense that programme your subconscious for success. You will find that if repeated each time you are at Foundation they will gain in strength. The relaxed state is the ideal time for repeating them to yourself. You can use them in your own way, either before entering your house or afterwards, or even repeating some before and some after. However you do it, it is recommended you set a pattern and generally stick with it.

Remember, practising this relaxation is a way of life that will bring the benefits you desire. I strongly recommend three sessions a day – one in the morning, one in the afternoon and the third in the evening. It is better to practise for three sessions of 5 minutes than one of 15. Obviously the more you do the better the results, it really is up to you. The deep relaxation combined with the techniques that follow in the next few chapters will give you the edge. I cannot recommend it to you enough and, as you know, 'It Only Works!'

Summary

1. Practise the deep relaxation in conjunction with the exercises in this book in order to manage your stress.
2. Visit your House on the Right Bank and ensure Quality Recovery Time. Practise at least once per day, although three times a day will maximize your benefits. Three sessions of 5 minutes will be better for you than one session of 15 minutes.

6

The Entrance Vestibule, the Conditioning Gym and the Central Hallway

Reactions to the Basic Relaxation Technique

On the MindStore courses I usually combine the Simple Relaxation exercise and the first House on the Red Bank exercise (see Chapter 5) into one, calling it the Foundation Exercise. It lasts about 40 minutes and at the end of it the vast majority doing it for the first time with me cannot believe that 40 minutes have passed. Many are convinced that 10 or at the most 15 minutes have elapsed. In that deeply relaxed state time does not exist in the same way that we normally think of it.

I am sure you can think of a time when you have got into bed and fallen asleep almost the moment your head hit the pillow, to find when you wake up 7, 8 or 9 hours later that you just cannot believe you've been asleep that long, that you are convinced you have been asleep for only minutes. Likewise I know that if I am out jogging I can often drift into a wonderful day-dreamy state where again my perception of time becomes distorted and I don't notice the strides go by.

This is often talked about by the greats of sport. Timothy Gallwey in his excellent *Inner Game* books draws attention to this. He describes it as 'the white moment'. I remember Yvonne Murray, the great British athlete, explain at a seminar I ran for the Scottish Rugby Squad in 1992 that when she won her gold medal at the European Championships something similar happened. She told us that as she ran the 3,000 metres final she was aware of everything until she hit the final 100 metres – then, she said, it all seemed to go white and all she was aware of was her own breathing until she hit the tape and it all came back again.

I was recently sent a copy of a video by a good friend. It was from a golf programme about great memories from that wonderful sport. The 1964 US Open Champion Ken Ventura described how on the last couple of holes of the penultimate round he went all 'glassy' and was sweating all over. At the end of the round a doctor told him not to play in the final round. He played the final round anyway and now says that he cannot remember anything about the round, that he has never been able to remember anything about it. At the eighteenth green he can remember Ray Floyd, then 21 years old, picking Ken's ball out of the hole and giving it to him. Ray was in tears, Ken also broke down and he then looked at Ray's score card – Ken had not filled in one single holes score, there were no numbers on it and to this day Ken cannot remember one of Ray's shots that day.

Many sporting greats have talked about the special state they seem to get into when they can do no wrong, when everything is perfect. Timothy Gallwey describes tennis players experiencing the ball coming at them in slow motion over the net. They are in peak state.

Over the years I've spent travelling around the country teaching the MindStore course, many people have approached me and told me of car accidents they have been in at some time in their past. They all describe it as happening as if in slow motion.

Perhaps, in this special state of mind, time is experienced

in a different way. Maybe we can use this to our advantage. In Chapter 9 I will come back to this and describe the possibilities for using it in more detail.

Other observations people have made when they first try this Foundation Exercise include feelings in the limbs of heaviness or lightness but different, a pleasant relaxed feeling especially in the arms and hands. We know that this state is a healthy one, that the heart beat slows down and the blood vessels dilate allowing the blood to reach parts that may not have had a quality flow for some time. Working with physiotherapists in football, I've found that they prefer their subjects to be totally relaxed. They say it helps the subjects to recover better, and that makes sense to me.

Some people experience an itchiness as the blood apparently reaches those parts that have not had it for sometime. Some salivate more (I know I do) some even fall into a comfortable sleep. Many sense a different awareness – they seem more creative as ideas come to assist in their problem-solving.

In reality the autonomic nervous system does experience change while you are using the relaxation techniques. The sympathetic nervous system controlling the heart rate, respiratory rate, body temperature, digestion, blood-pressure and muscular activity slows down. This relaxation response brings the parasympathetic branch of the nervous system into play, lowering oxygen consumption, blood-pressure and the levels of lactic acid and cortisone. It causes the internal organs to work more efficiently.

In the brain there is an increase in mood-changing biochemistry with the production of neurotransmitters and an increase in serotonin throughout the body, inducing a sense of calm and even happiness.

The Electroencephalogram, or EEG, picks up brainwave

activity which corresponds to different states of being:

Wide awake	Beta waves
Day-dream	Alpha waves
Light sleep	Theta waves
Deep sleep	Delta waves

Delta rhythms exist when we are asleep. Theta is a light, sleepy, dreamlike state. Alpha a deep physically relaxed state of emotional calm, even day-dreaming. Beta is the wide-awake day-to-day conscious state.

The state people reach in the physical and mental Foundation level of the MindStore techniques produces a predominance of alpha and theta rhythms.

Foundation and the MindStore techniques will impact your health and, as you will learn, your entire life, your relationships, your career – indeed any aspect of life you care to focus on.

The challenge we have, though, is fitting it into the packed routine of daily living. I do not take 40 minutes in one session in my day, I, like you, don't have that luxury – however 10 or 15 minutes is quite easy to find – you will be surprised. As you become more used to taking time to practise you will become more efficient and reach the level of Foundation you desire quickly. May I point out here that we do need QRT – Quality Recovery Time – so make sure you allow yourself however much time you need to practise.

In our next session, Exercise 3, you will again physically relax as before, and once on the right bank you will imagine walking towards your house there. You will return to the entrance area, you will open the door and you will step inside. You will immediately create what we will call the Entrance Vestibule. As you continue to develop your right-brain faculties you will decide on the shape, the walls, the flooring, the decorative features and lighting. It is important to be creative at this stage, to imagine a welcoming, attractive space.

Since the MindStore techniques will give you tools for reaching much more of your potential you may wish to erect somewhere within the entrance vestibule a symbol of your potential. Something that might have meaning for you as you become the person you wish to be. Clearly the symbols of success in sport, music and the stage might be obvious, but what would you have?

I have a symbol representing my family, it's a three-dimensional holographic image of Norma, Anthony, Christopher and myself. We are healthy, happy and prosperous. I am often away travelling and I find that this symbols always rekindles my desire to do my very best. I find it motivates me to do whatever has to be done. Trust what comes to mind. If nothing comes, just leave it until you do think of something sometime in the future.

As the Entrance Vestibule will lead to the many rooms within and the tools there, it is important that you make the entrance area welcoming, warm and attractive. You will find that you will become more creative as you continue to practise, so do not be too judgemental about your first mental efforts, you can add to them in due course.

Next we will create the Conditioning Gym. As the name suggests it conditions us or prepares us for the rest of the rooms within the house.

The use of this imaginary gymnasium is a vital part of the

techniques, because it helps us with our personal

Personal Energy

As we travel through our day we can all too easily add to the luggage of life. For many the events of a day add their own stresses and strains which take their toll on personal energy and, depending on an individual's reaction, can produce negative mindsets, mood changes, even depressed feelings and attitudes. For some all it takes is one throwaway negative comment by a colleague or friend to send the mind and body on the downward slope of the spiral of negativity.

How often has it happened to you? You've had a good day, everything has gone well. Maybe you have been involved with a particular activity with someone you have only recently met, either in your job or within a friendship group. Together you have been fully engaged, perhaps involving others but you have achieved what you set out to and to the very best of your ability, indeed you have succeeded. As the day comes to a close a friend informs you that throughout the day you addressed the new person by the wrong name. It was a simple error, he or she didn't say anything and probably understood, not feeling the need to embarrass you or even bother with it. All of a sudden, though, you completely focus on the negative, you start to process all manner of put-downs, you introduce self-doubt, you feel a fool and the good of the day seems completely lost.

Many of us get to the evening and the day has drained us. The family or friends may have been looking forward to something important happening that evening and you just can't find the energy. Other nights you seem to have all the energy you need to engage in whatever you need to or want to.

A lack of energy can have a major negative impact on our lives, it may cause us to miss out on enjoyable activities or opportunities that can provide for our growth and development, or simply to miss out on the enjoyment of life.

The tools of the Conditioning Gym become very important then. First we will construct a showering area that we will use to create 'instant state change', where we can drain away the effects of the day and replace any negativity with a vibrant and positive expectation. My idea here is to use the obvious symbology of cleansing to reinforce the positive messages we will give ourselves. Once again, with MindStore we will establish a pattern of thought that, through repetition, will automatically gain importance in its meaning and trigger the desired results.

You will create a shower head that when turned on will provide, in your imagination, a warm flow of spring water. This water will gently run through your hair and down over every inch of your body, which I suggest drains away mental fatigue while restoring vibrant life. Also the shower will produce bright sunlight, which you can imagine piercing into your brain and filtering out all the negativity that has been building up. I strongly recommend releasing any sense of lack – in your self or your ability, opportunity, self-image or application. You can focus on classic human traits such as fear, pettiness, anger, envy or greed and just imagine them all being washed away.

Simply drain away the negative build-up of the day. I strongly recommend doing this in the evening before or after your meal. It will set you up for the rest of your time before sleep. You will find that you will become refreshed with

77

abundant energy to enjoy your evening to the full. We will take this imaginary shower before entering the rest of the house and it will become a part of the Standard Entry Exercise of the MindStore techniques.

Now I strongly recommend that you fully engage your creativity with regard to the showering area. Make it a very special feature of your house, not just a simple little showering cubicle but something outstanding in design and layout. I have beautiful marble pillars and tiling – and my shower head is way up on a cliff edge! A large rustic door winds up slowly to allow a waterfall to pour all over me, so refreshing and enjoyable in my imagination.

Then, turning off the flow, you step out of the area instantly dried and fresh with a positive commitment and expectation of what is to come. We will do this before moving on to the rooms within. It is not recommended to enter into the techniques that come later with a negative attitude. We can recognize that we may have a challenge to deal with, however our expectation is that we will tackle it and expect a solution.

Within the Conditioning Gym we have another powerful programming tool: the Energizing Beam. Many participants on MindStore courses are quite amazed with the results they can get from this simple idea. Here we will imagine an Energizing Beam that rises from a platform. We will stand on the platform to pretend we are charging ourselves up with a vibrating beam of energy that will rise through the body and on up to the scalp.

The Energizing Beam will release you from the manifestations of stress and provide you with a tool for instantly increasing your personal energy. Thousands of us use the beam to manage, for example, headaches, the first symptoms of a cold, even that feeling of falling asleep at the wheel while driving at night or on long journeys.

The technique here is first of all to admit the reality of any physical complaint to yourself, not to deny the symptoms. Saying to yourself over and over again 'I do not have a headache' is not the answer. Admit to yourself, for example, 'I have a headache but I don't want it.' Close your eyes, take three deep breaths then relax your body from your head to your toes. Then adjust your awareness and focus your imagination on being at the right bank of the river. Imagine the lush green grass, the blue sky and the sounds of the landscape before you look towards your house with the red roof. Go forward and enter your house by the Entrance Vestibule, past your symbol of potential and on into your Conditioning Gym. Have a good shower, then stand on your Energizing Beam. Admit your condition (e.g. headache, cold symptoms, fatigue, etc.) but tell yourself you don't want to be this way. Turn on the Energizing Beam and imagine the healthy and energetic vibration rise from below your feet on up your body and into your brain. Leave the house and return to the river's edge, telling yourself that you will count from 1 to 7 and that when you get to 7 this will be gone. Count then from 1 to 4 – at 4 remind yourself that you are beyond the midpoint, already feeling better – and when you get to 7 open your eyes and become both physically and mentally alert and in perfect health. At 5 begin to adjust your body; at 6 prepare to open your eyes; and at 7 open your eyes and mentally say to yourself 'I am wide awake both physically and mentally alert.'

You will find by focusing your thoughts on whatever you have to do the condition will have gone. Most of these conditions are just the manifestation of stress, and since relaxation is the only real natural cure for stress the fact that you go through the above routine will take care of the stress anyway.

By further reinforcing your intention in the Alpha/Theta state you give a powerful message to the brain to produce the outcome you want. It is as if the bio-computer is in its maximum condition for receiving and acting on input.

This routine of three deep breaths followed by the head-to-toe relaxation and the focus of imagination on the Right Bank before entering your house we call the Standard Entry Exercise.

You will find that you can use your Energizing Beam to increase your energy dramatically. You can use it in the evening after a busy day, to end a QRT session, before or after your meal. Its applications are endless: before a party, a meeting, sport or a presentation; after a long journey – indeed any time you need that extra surge of OOMPH.

I personally would never dream of standing up and giving a presentation or speech without first of all taking a full relaxation in order to focus my mind and body on the task before me. To end the session with a charge on my Energizing Beam sets me up with an abundance of vitality that often takes my audience quite by surprise. I recommend its use fully to you. Its immediate benefits will be obvious, and the long-term results are even more significant. Course participants have reported back that by combining the relaxation with both the shower and the beam they have gained control over illness and conditions such as hypertension, shingles, and various aches and pains.

Once again, *'It Only Works'* – make it a way of life and you will enjoy so much more of your life. Remember, showering before going further into your House on the Right Bank is an important part of the Standard Entry Exercise and therefore another step in the MindStore process.

Now, when you are ready go through this third exercise to construct your Entrance Vestibule and Conditioning Gym. You will imagine taking a shower but we will leave the use of your Energizing Beam until later. Again you may find you get best results by first recording the exercise and playing it back to yourself or by having a friend read it to you.

EXERCISE 3 — THE ENTRANCE VESTIBULE AND THE CONDITIONING GYM

Find a comfortable position in your chair, close your eyes and begin breathing in a regular and slow manner. We will now begin to focus your mind and body on relaxing into a healthy state of being. Once again, as I mention each part of your body concentrate on it and focus your thinking on producing relaxation.

Take a deep breath and relax...take another deep breath and relax...take a deep breath and again relax... My scalp is relaxed, I feel my scalp relaxed... My forehead is relaxed, I feel my forehead relaxed... My eyelids are relaxed, I feel my eyelids relaxed... My face is relaxed, I feel my face relaxed... My tongue is relaxed, I feel my tongue relaxed... My jaw is relaxed, I feel my jaw relaxed... My throat is relaxed, I feel my throat relaxed...

My shoulders are relaxed, I feel my shoulders relaxed... My arms and hands are relaxed, I feel my arms and hands relaxed... My upper back is relaxed, I feel my upper back relaxed... My chest is relaxed, I feel my chest relaxed... My lower back is relaxed, I feel my lower back relaxed...

My abdomen is relaxed, I feel my abdomen relaxed...

81

My hips are relaxed, I feel my hips relaxed... My thighs are relaxed, I feel my thighs relaxed... My knees are relaxed, I feel my knees relaxed... My calves are relaxed, I feel my calves relaxed... My ankles are relaxed, I feel my ankles relaxed... My toes are relaxed, I feel my toes relaxed... My soles are relaxed, I feel my toes relaxed... My heels are relaxed, I feel my heels relaxed...

Take a deep breath and relax...

I will now imagine that I am in a very special place of relaxation... I fully pretend that I am there...I will give myself a short period to fully engage in this and enjoy it [30 seconds approx.].

Take a deep breath and relax...

I will now adjust and imagine that I am standing on the river bank... The river is behind me and I am facing a wonderful landscape...

I can feel my feet on the lush green grass...overhead the sky is deep blue and the air is fresh with the scent of the meadow...I can hear the sounds of the wonderful landscape before me...

I now look towards my house and remind myself of its construction, the features of the walls, the red roof and the entrance area... I move forward now to stand at the entrance...in a moment I will open the door to create my Entrance Vestibule and to place there a symbol of my potential...

I now open the door...first of all I create the shape of this room and the height of the ceiling...now the decorative features, colours and lighting... In a moment I will place here a symbol of my potential, I will trust my creativity and what comes to mind... I will pass through the Entrance Vestibule in all future exercises as part of the Standard Entry Exercise. I am programming at Foundation level. In a moment I will create my Conditioning Gym... A room I will use for the fine-tuning of my energy and for relief from the manifestations of stress...

The Conditioning Gym is attached to the Entrance Vestibule... I now create the shape of the room and the height of the ceiling...now the decorative features, colours and lighting... I will now install a showering area for cleansing negative energy and its underlying destructive thought patterns... I decide on its shape and dimensions...I select its colours...I now place its shower head and a control unit for regulating its flow... I will use this showering area in all future exercises and practice sessions...

In a moment I will stand within my shower and cleanse away any current negativity and underlying thought patterns...

I now enter my showering area and turn on the flow in order that its imaginary cleansing action can commence... I pretend to feel the warm spring waters run through my hair and down over every inch of my body, draining away mental fatigue and restoring vibrant life in its wake...

I now imagine the bright sunlight reaching deep within...filtering out and washing away all my limiting and destructive attitudes, particularly my negative thinking today...

Readjusting and turning off the shower I now step out, instantly dried and fresh with positive expectations...

I will now create my Energizing Beam that will have its source rise from a platform on the floor... I will use this vibrating beam to take away the physical manifestations of stress and for instant access to increased personal energy...

I have now created my Conditioning Gym...it will become an integral part of my MindStore techniques as I make them an important part of my life. I will now recite my positive affirmations [e.g. I now release myself from all negativity at all levels in my life/I now decide to think bright, happy and positive thoughts at all times/Every day and in every way I get better and better]...

I will now leave my house and return to the river's edge... I feel the lush green grass beneath my feet. I will shortly count from 1 to 7 and gradually adjust to come out of this healthy state of deep relaxation...

1...2...3...4...now beyond the midpoint, when I open my eyes I will be wide awake and revitalized both physically and mentally...5, I begin to adjust my body...6, I prepare to open my eyes...and 7, I open my eyes, wide awake now, both physically and mentally alert.

The Central Hallway

The Central Hallway is the area of your house you will enter immediately you leave the Conditioning Gym on all future exercises and practice sessions. As you might expect this hallway leads to all the other possible rooms in your house. Once again the layout of this area is up to you and your creativity, and once again decide to make it attractive and bright. You will decide on the shape, the height of the ceiling and the decorative features. You could choose spiralling staircases or a wide spacious room with vast ornate ceilings and fantastic pillars. It is all up to you.

One day at a course I was teaching in Glasgow a friend and colleague from my days in Social Work was participating. She came out to have a chat and then shared with me her personal observation that had a profound impact on me and, as it seemed, on her too.

I always ask participants on the courses to thank themselves for the quality of their thinking at the end of each exercise. She told me with a tear in her eye just how much she appreciated this since it was the first time she actually thanked herself for anything. She reflected that all too easily she had regularly put herself down but had never praised herself nor appreciated just how special she really was. I can tell you that many other colleagues and friends had recognized her contributions and indeed were grateful for her commitment, skill and friendship.

We both realized that hers was not an isolated experience and, since I had spent many years worrying about my health, we suddenly understood that many, many people – indeed probably the vast majority – engage in personal put-downs with ease yet possibly never actually praise themselves or appreciate themselves for anything.

With this in mind I decided to add to the construction of the Central Hallway. It will, after all, lead to the rest of the rooms in your house and will have to be passed through on the way to them. Since you will find it when you are in the deep yet powerful Alpha/Theta state of relaxation it could be used to raise your consciousness on the positive to overcome any negative self-image that you may have. I am sure that if you choose to, you can remember times when you have done your very best, when you have achieved or experienced the joy of life.

Let's, in constructing our Central Hallway, place up on the walls images depicting times from our past when we have been at our very best. You can place there murals, painting and photographs – hugely big images from those special moments. Trust what comes to mind. By renewing them at the Alpha/Theta level you will be restating to yourself that you can achieve, that you have experienced joy and happiness in the past and that, of course, you can expect to in the future. Such a simple idea could potentially have a massive impact on your self-esteem and therefore on your day-to-day experience.

I myself selected early childhood memories of fun and

achievement – scoring a goal for my primary school football team; a 40-foot put on the golf course; the birth of my sons; a standing ovation from an appreciative audience and many more. Take time to think about this and choose what you will put on the walls of your Hallway. These images are yours and have meaning to you, do not judge them against what you might think others place there. Have fun, have a go, sometimes the simplest ideas are the best.

Exercise 4 – The Central Hallway

Find a comfortable position in your chair, close your eyes and begin breathing in a regular and slow manner. We will now begin to focus your mind and body on relaxing into a healthy state of being. Once again, as I mention each part of your body concentrate on it and focus your thinking on producing relaxation.

Take a deep breath and relax...take another deep breath and relax...take a deep breath and again relax... My scalp is relaxed, I feel my scalp relaxed... My forehead is relaxed, I feel my forehead relaxed... My eyelids are relaxed, I feel my eyelids relaxed... My face is relaxed, I feel my face relaxed... My tongue is relaxed, I feel my tongue relaxed... My jaw is relaxed, I feel my jaw relaxed... My throat is relaxed, I feel my throat relaxed...

My shoulders are relaxed, I feel my shoulders relaxed... My arms and hands are relaxed, I feel my arms and hands relaxed... My upper back is relaxed, I feel my upper back relaxed... My chest is relaxed, I feel my chest relaxed... My lower back is relaxed, I feel my lower back relaxed...

My abdomen is relaxed, I feel my abdomen relaxed...
My hips are relaxed, I feel my hips relaxed... My
thighs are relaxed, I feel my thighs relaxed... My knees
are relaxed, I feel my knees relaxed... My calves are
relaxed, I feel my calves relaxed... My ankles are
relaxed, I feels my ankles relaxed... My toes are
relaxed, I feel my toes relaxed... My soles are relaxed, I
feel my soles relaxed... My heels are relaxed, I feel my
heels relaxed...

Take a deep breath and relax... I will now imagine that
I am in a very special place of relaxation... I fully
pretend that I am there...I will give myself a short
period to fully engage in this and enjoy it [30 seconds].

Take a deep breath and relax...I will now adjust and
imagine that I am standing on the river bank...the river
is behind me and I am facing into a wonderful
landscape...

I can feel my feet on the lush green grass...overhead
the sky is deep blue and the air is fresh with the scent
of the meadow...I can hear the sounds of the wonderful
landscape before me...

I now move forward and into my Entrance Vestibule,
past my symbol of potential and on into my
Conditioning Gym...

In a moment I will stand within my shower and cleanse
away any current negativity...

I now enter my showering area and turn on the flow in order that its imaginary cleansing action can commence... I pretend to feel the warm spring waters run through my hair and down over every inch of my body, draining away mental fatigue and restoring vibrant life in its wake...

I now imagine the bright sunlight reaching deep within, filtering out and washing away all my limiting and destructive attitudes, particularly my negative thinking today...

Readjusting and turning off the shower I now step out, instantly dried and fresh with positive expectations....

In a moment I will create my Central Hallway... This leads to all the other rooms of my inner home and is accessed directly from the Conditioning Gym... I now create its shape and the height of the ceiling... Now the decorative features, colours and lighting...

On the wall I will now place images depicting time from my past when I have been at my very best...[1 minute approx.]

I have now created my Central Hallway...it leads to all the other rooms in my inner home...

I will now leave my house and return to the river's edge...I feel the lush green grass beneath my feet. I will shortly count from 1 to 7 and gradually adjust to come out of this healthy state of deep relaxation...

1...2...3...4...now beyond the midpoint, when I open my eyes I will be wide awake and revitalized both physically and mentally...5, I begin to adjust my body...6, I prepare to open my eyes...and 7, I open my eyes and am wide awake now, both physically and mentally alert.

Summary

1. Deep physical and mental relaxation provides the healthy response to the effects of stress.
2. Brain wave activity is lowered in relaxation.
3. The Symbol of Potential will reinforce your belief that you can achieve much more in your life.
4. Use your Conditioning Gym to manage your physical energy constantly.
5. A very good time to practise is in the evening as an inter-phase between the demands of the day and your night-time activity.
6. The Standard Entry Exercise:
   a) Find a comfortable position, close your eyes, take three deep breaths and with each exhalation relax.

   b) Relax your body from head to toes e.g. my scalp is relaxed, I feel my scalp relax; my forehead is relaxed, I feel my forehead relax, etc.

   c) Imagine being on the river bank, go forward and enter

your house by the Entrance Vestibule before having a shower in your Conditioning Gym.

7. Build your self-esteem by placing positive images on the wall of your Central Hallway.
8. You are a very special person and throughout your life there have been moments when you have demonstrated just how wonderful you really are.

Goal-setting and Problem-solving

Until one is committed there is the chance to draw back;
always ineffectiveness. Concerning all acts of initiative (and
creation) there is one elementary truth, the ignorance of which
kills countless ideas and splendid plans; – that the moment one
definitely commits oneself, then providence moves too.
All sorts of things occur to help one that would not otherwise
have occurred. A whole stream of events issues from the decision
raising in one's favour all manner of unforeseen incidents and
meetings and material assistance which no man could have
dreamt would come his way. Whatever you can do, or dream
you can, begin it!
Boldness has genius, magic and power in it.
Begin It Now.

GOETHE

A great genius of a thinker sums up in a few lines what many have attempted to explain in books and training programmes. This almost magnetic and seemingly hidden force has been ever-present in all the success stories I have read about or researched.

The great joy for all of us on the MindStore team is the constant letters, telephone calls and feedback we receive at courses. Many say, 'It has changed my life!' and although that's quite a statement to make I understand what they mean because it has completely changed mine.

I think what really has this impact is a combination of releasing negativity and becoming positive while at the same time fully understanding and committing our thoughts and energy to the information we are about to cover. This material has to be among the most important information you can ever come across. Many approaching it are expecting complicated ideas and are often disappointed and even choose to deny that what can really make the difference in your life is so simple.

In his great book *Think and Grow Rich* Napoleon Hill attempts to forewarn his readers of the power that can be harnessed when the secret of what lies behind all success is discovered. He doesn't come right out with it, he leaves the reader to discern from the pages that follow what it is, and of course many fail to see it because it is so obvious it is paradoxically easily missed.

It's been my joy to hear from those who have accepted my explanation and who have put our techniques to use. Their growth and satisfying achievement are so encouraging. Yet others, often in the same office or family, think it is a 'load of rubbish'. It's sad but of course they are absolutely correct – whatever you believe will be true as far as your brain is concerned. So choosing to accept these ideas and put them into practice will *only work*; on the other hand, dismiss them and you will be equally correct. You see, your response is up to you and you will determine your own outcomes.

I actually believe that if you are reading this book and have come this far then you do want to gain from reading through these pages. Your desire to learn and find out is enough to get things going. Please do all you can to understand what I am about to explain and get to work with it. I wish you well.

Setting a Goal and Writing it Down

My life took a dramatic surge forward when I read a story about Yale University. I read that in 1953 the University carried out a piece of research among the final-year students to find out what they thought about that great seat of learning. All the final-year students from all the university departments were interviewed. Apparently they were asked to give their opinion on the campus, the staff, the academic facilities, the library, the lecture theatres, lecturers, courses – even the food and ancillary services. Everything that could be imagined was asked; the questionnaire also asked them questions about life in general.

As I read on I discovered that one of the questions they asked was – 'Do you have goals?' It seems that 10 per cent of the total said yes to this. That in itself did not impact me, at this point I was simply engaged in reading and taking it all in. The next question I read – 'If you have goals, do you have them written down?' Apparently 4 per cent of the total said 'Yes' to this. Again I wasn't particularly taken aback, I just read on.

Twenty years later, in 1973, the University were about to repeat the exercise by questioning the then final-year students on roughly the same type of information. I suppose in effect this was a good consumer questionnaire or market research project. In coming to their decision to go ahead someone objected and asked that the commitment be made to find all who had left 20 years before and to find out where they were in their lives now. This was agreed and the search spanned all areas of the world; some former students had died but it is reckoned that the vast majority were found and their questionnaires completed.

What I now learned stopped me in my tracks and had a profound impact on my thinking – to be honest, it changed my life forever. I read that the 4 per cent who had written down their goals all those years before were streets ahead of all the rest when it came to indications that might suggest success. Their wheel of life was in balance, with high scores. Their well-being, commitment to their community, their relationships and much more were just so outstandingly different from the rest. One statistic that had a big impact on me was that apparently each individual within the 4 per cent was financially secure, indeed they were worth more than the other 96 per cent – those who did not write down their goals – put together.

Working as a community worker in a large peripheral housing scheme in Glasgow I found this to be quite disturbing. I had spent years working with the unfortunates who had difficulty coping in such an environment. There were many good things that we had achieved together, but the above information caused me to question everything.

Surely, I thought, it's not as simple as setting a goal and writing it down. It dawned on me that tucked away in my head I had had some dreams of achievement as a child and even as an adult some fanciful ideas of things I would like to do, but I had very rarely brought them to the forefront of my mind. I certainly had never written them down. I was practising the writing of objectives and plans for my job, but more often than not annual plans and the like were more about keeping bosses happy or making an impression. The Yale experience was different and it set me off on a great adventure. Indeed I am still on the journey and it has been so exciting.

I also focused on the fact that in '53 10 per cent claimed to have goals but that 60 per cent of these didn't bother to write them down. Perhaps the psychological power of going to the trouble to do this meant some kind of commitment. Could this be part of what Goethe meant?

Apart from my job at this time I also had an embryonic travel business that's main focus was on skiing. I had certainly addressed the issues of cash-flow projections and profit and loss accounts, and the sense of risk in running a business had thrown up the natural fears of 'What if it all goes wrong?', 'What if I go bankrupt?', etc. Suddenly right before me was a way forward, so simple yet, if it were true and worked for me, then I was surely off and running.

I made a commitment to find out as much as I could about this goal-setting thing. It became clear from what I was reading that it was big. Many metaphors were used to explain it all. Some talked about life being a game with spectators and players. The spectators were in the vast majority, observing from the sidelines, good at talking and giving opinions but never actually getting off their backsides to play. The players were the ones who seemed to live life to the full, who set and scored their goals.

Others talked in terms of there being rules to the game of life but that very few players knew what these were. It seemed to be a big secret but those who were in on it were the great successes, the winners and the achievers. It seemed that the hidden rule or great secret was simply to write down your goals.

Remember Frank Dick, the former Director of Coaching for British Athletics, and his idea of Mountain people and Valley people? Yet another metaphor: the Mountain people take the risk to win, setting their sights on the high ground in life and setting off in pursuit.

I like to think of the 'Ocean of Life'. On the ocean we all

have a chance, we are all in our very own boat. Provided we are born with no mental disability then surely we have a chance to make something of this life. (I am sure you will agree that many people with great physical disabilities can put most of us to shame when it comes to overcoming adversity and achieving.)

As I see it, out on the Ocean of Life there are storms and calm, rough seas and smooth, mirror-like surfaces. Life does have its ups and downs as the boat cuts through the water – the 4 per cent are the ones who know that you must have a rudder and an engine, while the 96 per cent don't even know these exist.

When the storms come – and come they do, especially the big one known as the recession – then even the 4 per cent can be blown off-course, but they seem to have the wherewithal to dig in, hold on to the rudder and turn on the engine to fight to get back on course to their destination. Incidentally, I have never met or read about anyone who got instant success, the journey is always rough, fraught with disappointment and apparent failure. Somehow those who do succeed just keep on going.

In the storm the 96 per cent without rudders and no engine are at the mercy of the wind and tide. They are blown all over the place. Sometimes in their lives a big ship comes close by. They attempt to cling on behind, hoping they can hitch a ride to the horizon, however the wake from the 4 per cent is usually too strong and they end up letting go.

When the calm comes, the 4 per cent efficiently turn on the engine and steam right on to their goal. In the calm the 96 per cent drift on in whatever current they find themselves.

I have a passion for this great truth, a truth I was never taught at school, college or university. I don't remember any time at all being spent on this, indeed I found out about it, like most people, quite by accident. I believe this must become a key part of the curriculum for every boy and girl. I can only marvel at what might have been for me and so many of my friends if this had been taught to us as a way of life. If only our socialization had this as a cornerstone.

As I see it, the 96 per cent of our population who really do not understand the importance of goals spend their entire lives helping and assisting the 4 per cent achieve their goals. This is one of life's greatest challenges and greatest truths. People who set goals always, just as Goethe implied, attract people, places and opportunities to them as if by some imaginary magnetic force. However it happens, it is my commitment to teach as many people as I can that they must engage in creating their own futures – lest others create them for them.

I often think of it as struggling to walk through thick mud throughout your life – up to your waist in it, moving ever so slowly and with great effort. Once goal-setting is understood it's as though you are plucked out of the mud and onto dry land. The mud still clings at first and hampers movement. You still move slowly but with a new enthusiasm. Then the mud begins to dry out, slowly, over time. You start to move a little faster, soon the mud cracks and begins to fall away. The pace quickens, you can now walk easily. You start to take bigger strides, now jogging before running and taking off.

All whom I have met who understand the nature of this great energy have witnessed how it starts as little drips of opportunity and breakthroughs, apparent signs of success coming few and far between. Then, in time, the drips become a tiny little flow, like a tap turned on just a bit and no more – slight yet constant reinforcement that all is beginning to show fruit. In time the tap flows with more force, then in full flush the flow becomes a stream, a river and finally an estuary in flood.

I cannot guarantee that by using the MindStore techniques life can change for the better all at once, but putting them into practice does *only* work. Thousands and thousands know of their potency. I believe that you couldn't cope if success came in an instant, you would be drowned and your life destroyed. No – you have to learn to adjust through time before the great gifts come their way. However, what I can assure you of is that the journey to your destination is actually what it is all about.

You must stop and smell the roses, to take in the roadside wonders, to enjoy the vista and the marvel of each step. Many know only too well that actually achieving a goal can become a great anticlimax. It's the desire for it and the excitement of moving towards it that give us all that zest for life. My own experience and my observation of others suggests that when a goal is achieved we are at our most vulnerable; another goal has to be found, and quickly. Otherwise we sit on our laurels and fade away.

The flower bud that brightens a summer's day bears the tiniest of potential fruit, which grows and ripens till its peak then falls to the ground to begin its decay until it is gone.

Many have said it better than I, but a man or woman without a goal is rotting away. The life expectancy after retirement is far too short unless a new focus can be found and commitment made to it.

Goal-setting and getting down to achieving the goals we set, no matter what gets in the way, is actually the stuff of life itself.

My searching and researching to understand it all has been more than interesting. I soon found that from time began those who achieved – whether in personal endeavour, exploration, invention, art, sport or business – all have understood the importance of knowing where you want to get to.

The greatest gift in life is the ability to think great thoughts and to have the strength to take action so those thoughts become reality in this wonderful and abundant world. Those who achieve this are those who take action.

Four Steps Forward

In attempting to find a model or a way forward for others, many have identified the simple steps that need to be taken. To put it as straightforwardly as possible, these steps are:

ONE Focus on a vision of what you want to achieve.
TWO Make your commitment to the vision.
THREE Plan out how you will get there.
FOUR Begin and take action.

Some add that a regular review (of progress) and adjustment process is vital on the way to the goal.

What is interesting is that these steps involve first of all the faculties of the right brain in bringing about an imagined outcome or goal. Then both brains have to merge to find the commitment, the vision plus a sense of what is possible. Then finally the left brain and its logic are brought into play to think through the plan.

Now clearly each of these steps is important, but what I have noticed – especially once I realized the importance of both brains and the dominance of the left, logical side – is that far

101

too much emphasis is put on the planning stage (Step Three) and often very little on fully focusing the mind on the vision (Step One). Indeed, because of the strength of the left brain's life experience, the right brain is hardly engaged by most of us and, as a result, the visions or goals we set are that much poorer.

I believe this is a major challenge for our lives today. All around us the fruits of the left-brain emphasis can be seen: lack of drive and commitment. The result? Mediocrity and lack of achievement.

Your Own Mission Statement

I remember listening to one of the great entrepreneurs, a man at the forefront of direct selling within the Life Assurance Industry. He was more than someone who had had a big dream and had pioneered his way to the top. He talked about the vision he still has and the great excitement he feels for what has yet to be done. He told me he wasn't the only one, there were others and it was a great time for all of them. He called himself and the others at the top Number Ones; around themselves they had attracted the Number Twos, Threes and Fours.

The Threes and Fours were the men and women with the management training who constantly searched for and demanded strategy and planning from top to bottom. He said that the Number Ones were no longer at the top, they had been replaced – initially by the Number Twos and eventually by the Threes and Fours. He felt, however, that the Threes and Fours no longer had a vision and indeed could not lead or inspire the troops. He actually feared for the future; he felt that new Number Ones – people whose vision of a bright, successful future is their primary motivation, without the over-emphasis on planning – would have to be found again.

I am not so well versed in the industry he came from, but I know what he was getting at. I have witnessed this throughout my years of spreading my message, particularly in the fields of industry and commerce.

One of the great trends of late has been the drive to concepts of Total Quality Management and the desire for empowered teams at all levels within a company. These are precious goals but all too often I have found people expressing doubts about the ability of expensive programmes to implement real change. The obvious starting point for most of our companies seems to be an attempt to restate a vision of the future through their Mission Statement. Many companies proudly have these Statements illuminated in their reception areas for all to read. Their publicity material is usually adorned with well-meaning words. I am not mocking this, but all too often when I ask employees (even fairly high-ranking ones) if they can recite the Mission Statement they usually shrug their shoulders and make some remark about it being a load of nonsense.

I believe that Mission Statements are important, but *all* the people within an organization must be able to feel that it is theirs, that they share ownership in their company's goals and visions. All to often this ownership is held only by those who write the Mission Statement and by those who feel they must pretend to endorse it in order to please the powers that be.

What is interesting, though, is the way in which many who seem to have no focus on the Mission are constantly engaged in strategy and planning to achieve it. If the plan looks impressive and has the right feel or flavour to it, then that's what it seems to be all about.

Business and industry training programmes tend to throw up the same old approaches, indeed the language used is all too familiar – yet by far the biggest problem, in my opinion, is that their emphasis gets hold of the wrong end of the stick.

Realistic and Achievable?

I am sure if you have come across goal-setting before then you will have heard some interesting words and phrases that seem to go with it. All too often, incidentally, those who teach it are far from passionate about explaining it, and when you attempt to find out what they themselves have achieved with this important tool you more often than not find their own results less than inspiring. As I am sure you have picked up by now, I believe the majority have got it all wrong.

You may have regularly heard people say that goals should be 'smart, stretching, exciting' but most usually 'realistic and achievable and of course measurable'. For me the most telling words here are *realistic* and *achievable*. These words and their meanings are driven by the logical drive of the dominant left brain. A brain that tends to look into the 'luggage of life' to ascertain what has been achieved before, what is possible and how it might be planned; then the goals are set. Of course such 'goals' will always be achievable and realistic.

Einstein said 'Imagination is more important than knowledge' – he was so correct. Imagination, rooted in the right brain, must lead the way in all goal-setting, for only it can see into wonderful futures of achievement and success. The left brain, steeped in knowledge, in other words the past, must then follow.

I came across a recording of Jackie Stewart, the great Scottish racing driver and inspiring ex-World Champion, giving a talk at a dinner for a marketing society. He spoke of the state of the car industry in the US some four years previously. He mentioned the trend in the market at that time regarding luxury and expensive cars. It seemed that Mercedes, BMWs, Porsches and Jaguars were far more popular with American car-buyers than the American makes. Indeed it was the desire of most Americans to own one of these makes; these cars were considered status symbols.

At this time a team from another company from outside the US and Europe, a company with no previous experience in this particular market, looked closely at it and decided to take it on. Their task was first to design and build a totally new car, then place it on the market and sell it in direct competition with these European models.

Their decision was to build one make and model of car only, not a range of models but simply a single car. Just think about this, think about how the left brain with its logic, reasoning and analysis must have viewed this task; just think what kind of vision must have been required to spur on such a project and then let the result sink in. For within 18 months of its introduction, the car was leading the US market, outselling all the BMWs, Mercedes and Jaguars put together.

What an awesome achievement – the car? The Lexus. And as I am writing this it is now the most popular luxury car in the entire world. Fantastic! Was the goal realistic and achievable? Of course not – at least, not by most people's standards of reality and possibility. I put it to you that such a goal would typically be thought of as impossible, unrealistic and in no way achievable. I put it to you that the vision was clear and powerful and made its mark, driving all the effort necessary to achieve it. Yes, planning, but only second to imagination.

We need the plans, but commitment to the goal is vital and must be the priority. The tendency is to put more energy into planning, understandable from a left-brain dominance point of view. Because of the emphasis on what's possible, achievable and realistic, the goals set are usually too small. Let me explain this in more detail because to me this must be understood before you can achieve any real results with the MindStore techniques.

COMFORT ZONES

One of the great challenges we face when we attempt to set goals is the impact of Comfort Zones, as mentioned in Chapter 3. Comfort Zones are relatively simple psychological models that help to explain human behaviour. We all have Comfort Zones about all aspects of our lives, and we tend to stay within them.

I have a particular Comfort Zone associated with speaking in public, whether that's to a handful of people or thousands in a conference theatre. I find the whole experience deeply pleasing and familiar. A Comfort Zone of your own might not come anywhere near mine in this area, but on the other hand you may be at absolute ease working with your computer where I choose to leave that to someone else.

We have Comfort Zones about everything. I have one as a father, a manager, a salesperson, as a cook, a husband; I have them for my golf, for painting, for playing music, etc. Teams have them, companies have them, towns have them and even countries have them. Once established they are very difficult to shake.

Take for example the golfer. Often those who enjoy the sport can find themselves playing on a fine summer's day when they can't really be bothered and are simply enjoying their time away from it all. Suddenly they find they have had a run of good shots, it's the 9th hole and their score is way below their best ever. If they keep this up, they realize, they will not only break their own record but maybe even the best in the club. However, this heightened sense of competitiveness paradoxically takes them out of their Comfort Zone. The result? As you might expect and what golfers know only too well, they soon begin to find the rough and bunkers and they miss the easiest of puts.

How often have you witnessed in other sports – for example in football – a team from the lower divisions leading by a goal in a cup competition, usually at home. They are beating a team from the top division, there are only minutes to go and suddenly there is a silly mistake, even a fluke and the big club equalizes. The minnow was out of its Comfort Zone and just had to fall back in again.

The Comfort Zone is certainly an interesting model, and of course when we are asked to improve on performance or take up a new task we can feel uncomfortable and prefer not to do whatever it is. A good friend from the financial services world talks about the 'adventure ground' being that area beyond the Comfort Zone. He puts it simply: 'To succeed we have to get out there and build new Comfort Zones.'

Evidence suggests that when we get out into the adventure ground we will tend to fall back into where we feel safe. My friend Mike explains how salespeople set monthly targets and in the first month many achieve it. He has noticed, however, that immediately they succeed, their drive and effort begin to fade away. They may begin to take time off or spend more time in the office rather than pushing on beyond what they believe is realistic and achievable in a month.

I often ask the audience to think about the down and outs and their Comfort Zones, about how much they perceive they are worth. If the down and out is given a gift of a pile of £10 notes, say £300 in one go, what do you expect him or her to do with it? Will he or she go to the bank and invest it or do all he or she can to get rid of it – quickly?

The challenge, though, is that we can never be absolutely clear about where our Comfort Zones actually exist. By setting your Wheel of Life you can get a reasonably good idea. Louis Tice, founder of the Pacific Institute in Seattle, talks about Comfort Zones being identified by self-esteem or self-image and current reality. Your current experience and self-confidence in a particular area of your life reflect, or at least give you an idea of, where your Comfort Zone might exist.

As I see it the power of the Comfort Zone to keep us where we are is the biggest single hurdle to moving forward and in particular to goal-setting and what can be achieved. If we follow the 'make them realistic and achievable' school then our goals will be set just beyond our present experience.

For example, the golfer on an 18 handicap aims to improve to 16. A person earning £25,000 aims to reach £27,000. A person living in a 2-bed semi desires to move up to a 3-bed semi. An employee aims to get a promotion up one level or one rung on the corporate ladder.

This all makes sense since the luggage of life and all the logical thought processes makes the idea of pushing out just a little bit from the Comfort Zone feel OK. It is stretching but can be achieved and, to be fair, is realistic. The desire to think it all through and of course plan out what has to be achieved on the way comes into play and in a sense confirms that, yes,

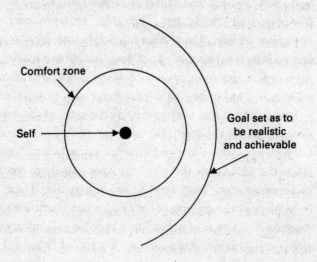

Comfort zone

Self

Goal set as to
be realistic
and achievable

the goal is possible, everybody is happy so let's get on with it.

The first steps are taken, well-meaning effort is expended, and some level of enthusiasm for the goal or outcome is found. Soon, however, procrastination sets in, the 'I'll do that tomorrow' or 'next week', and before you know it nothing much has changed and, well, you don't make the target – but at least you can say 'I got close'. On my travels around the country those who are caught up in this tend not to achieve.

Of course I am not exactly popular with those who are committed to the 'Science of Strategic Planning', especially in big businesses and the scores of consultants who encourage full plans and sophisticated models and programmes all laid out in advance.

You see, I like to keep things simple. My observation of those who do achieve and stand out for doing so don't seem

109

to do this 'realistic and achievable' thing backed up by all the planning and scheduling. The great entrepreneurs, world champion athletes, Oscar-winning actors, the great entertainers fascinate most people – I am passionate about reading about them or listening to them on chat shows, and best of all meeting with them and finding out at first-hand what makes them tick.

I tend to find that they give away the same clues about how they made it to the top. They very rarely find instant success, but a lot of commitment and drive has come before. They have taken the knocks on the way and have usually overcome big disappointments. They tend to say things like 'I was in the right place at the right time' or 'You make your own luck.' In most cases a vision of achieving a specific goal or target even from early childhood stands out. A sense of 'I knew I would one day do it' also makes an impression. Now, if this tends to be present in all success stories then surely it must have significance. Yet many seem to lack this vision, getting caught up instead in all that planning and preparation.

I get a great deal of pleasure from the cinema and watching good films. Many of them have had a big impact on me, as I am sure they have had on millions of others. One of the great movies, for me, is the film *Dead Poets Society* starring the genius Robin Williams. I usually start my course by drawing attention to his great line, 'Seize the day.' I tend to watch the BAFTA Awards, and of course the Oscars – I like to hear the speakers and the interviews afterwards with the winners; usually the same old gems come out about how they got to such levels of success. Al Pacino's acceptance speech in 1993, for his portrayal of a blind man in *Scent of a Woman*, was one of the greatest I have ever heard. His integrity and passion so impressed me as he spoke of his humble beginnings and his personal self-belief.

I will never forget Whoopi Goldberg winning her Oscar in 1990 and explaining how she had dreamt about it all her life. As far as I can make out, most people who succeed do say this kind of thing. Interesting? – maybe even important? It's *VITAL!* You see, your brain needs a vision for the future. Let's just look a bit closer at the significance of this kind of statement. If she genuinely dreamt of being an Oscar-winner all her life then she must have started as a small child. But let's just check out some facts here. She is black. Yes, black. Why am I drawing your attention to the fact? Well, because she was only the third black person to win an Oscar. Now I happen to think this is appalling but that's how life seems to be, maybe it will get better – let's all hope so. So she is black, she didn't come from a rich and famous family or, as one might think, the 'right side of town'. So if we think of her Comfort Zone as a child, her current reality and self-esteem then:

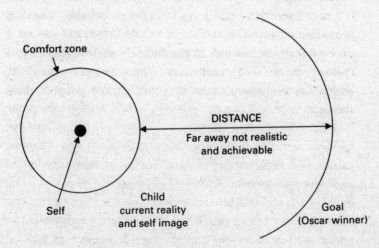

Her goal was not on the immediate horizon of her Comfort Zone as a child, it was a 'million miles' away. In terms of being realistic and achievable it was not (taken from what most people would term realistic and achievable). It certainly was not the kind of goal that popular thinking would suggest one should consider.

Think about it, if the people who say you should make your goals realistic and achievable had got hold of her as a child she would never have made it. None of us would ever have heard of her and we would have missed her great talent. You see she dared to dream – yes, as children do, but she made her commitment to it. I put it to you that such a dream and commitment drove her to her goal.

History is just littered with this 'I dreamt about it' experience, but what actually excites me most about this is something that is fundamental to the relationship between the starting point i.e. the Comfort Zone, and the outcome – the goal. It's not the fact that the goal is so far away from the starting point. It's not that it isn't really realistic and achievable. The big, important observation is: That as a child begins to look out at his or her dream set way in the future – and remember to a child the future seems such a very long time away – the child, in making the commitment to a goal cannot possibly think through

am I going to achieve it. The child doesn't really know, hasn't the faintest idea. There is usually not an ounce of evidence from the past or present that can support him or her, the big input here is the fact that the vision is clear, it excites the child and he or she really wants it. No child at this stage is concerned with the steps that have to be taken.

Such a force has brought children out of ghettos, abject poverty and the most challenging of situations slowly but surely to achieve the most fantastic outcomes. In sport, in art, on the stage, in film, in business, in science, in politics and on and on and on. And the one great truth is that the goal is BIG and they don't know HOW they will do it but they make their commitment to doing whatever it takes. Goethe was absolutely correct – 'a whole manner of unforeseen incidents and meetings and material assistance which no man could have dreamt would come his way. All sorts of things occur to help one.'

I recently spent a morning with Robert Heller, the author of some really outstanding business management books such as *The Super Managers* and *The Super Chiefs*. He agrees with me on the need for ownership of a big vision. He talked about Japan and its phenomenal success since the Second World War. He reflected on the fact that the country and its economy were absolutely wiped out. Japan has no natural resources, a com-

113

pletely unique language – there really wasn't much going for it. In the industries the Japanese chose to establish they faced almost complete monopoly from the IBMs of this world. To them, it would seem, there surely is no such thing as impossible.

I am sure you are beginning to get my point here. Please do not allow thoughts of 'but, but, you need to plan' or 'but it's all right for the children. I am now an adult and have long ago given up my dreams' or 'I haven't a clue what I would like to do with my life.' Don't let such thoughts get in your way here. This stuff works and will for you no matter your present situation, age, gender, etc. Just read on.

You see, when you set the goal on the immediate horizon of the Comfort Zone something interesting happens.

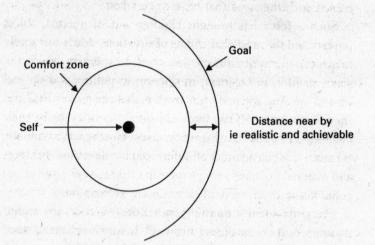

The goal feels realistic and achievable, you can usually start to plan out what has to be done immediately, indeed a step-by-step plan to success can be put together. I think what happens is that the conscious mind looks at the goal and, logically, from a 'luggage of life' point of view, can accept it. On the other hand, the subconscious looks at it and equally accepts that it is possible and leaves the responsibility for achieving it to the conscious mind.

This is where the challenge lies, because the conscious mind tends to be lazy, begins to produce procrastination and although you know what has to be done you put it off or eventually half-heartedly work it through, and generally the outcome is not up to expectations.

Let's look closer at those who set the big goals, well beyond current reality and Comfort Zones. 'I dreamt about this all my life' suggests a constant repetition, perhaps every night before sleep, even every morning, reminding oneself of the pleasures of achieving the goal. This constant repetition slips from the conscious activity of choosing to dream into the subconscious mind as a new Comfort Zone.

Current understanding of the subconscious suggests that the subconscious accepts all messages given to it from the conscious mind. It cannot distinguish between imagined ideas and apparent reality. If an idea is repeated enough then it will act on it. Going back to previous chapters we really do have to watch how and what we think. Our consistent thoughts produce our reality; to put it simply: 'Change what you think and change how you live.'

Since the dream is experienced in a present tense setting, i.e. the person choosing to dream about a successful outcome experiences it in the dream as though it were happening now, it sets up deep within a new Comfort Zone. We can presume then that the subconscious, accepting the new reality, looks out at the present reality and sees that the two don't match. It then has to get involved and bring the new reality about. It will cause people, places and opportunities to be attracted into

115

the life of the dreamer. If the vision is clear and precise then the person will become wide open to opportunities that would otherwise be missed.

This is really exciting, almost as though the planning and what has to be done to get to the goal will emerge on the journey. Ideas, contributions, actions and all other aspects of what has to be done will present themselves as and when required and in their own time – the correct time. But only if the vision is constantly viewed and the commitment to and belief in it are found.

Another, and yet even more exciting observation is this – this dreaming done at night or during moments in the day-dream state correspond to the presence of Alpha/Theta rhythms in the brain. What excites me is that those of us who gave up on our childhood dreams of fame and glory, or those of us who maybe never even started to think about setting goals, don't have to be over-concerned about dreaming for a lifetime. If we can access the Alpha/Theta state, and since time doesn't seem to exist there anyway, we can choose to structure visions or images of our future and ensure that they begin to happen, and quickly.

This is where a great deal of the excitement of what MindStore is about comes from. Participants learn how to bring about fantastic changes in their lives by using the techniques to create new Comfort Zones; by committing themselves to these new Comfort Zones, they succeed. The apparent magic of attracting people, places and opportunities, the endless coincidences as the journey bears fruit is what it's all about – it's absolutely wonderful.

I spend less time concerned about the plan and how am I going to get there than I do on making sure I am committed to a vision for my future. I apply this to all areas of my Wheel of Life. You see, by using this approach I have been able to build a very respectable and impressive client list. I have been able to work with the clients of my choice and find my way into situations and meet people that most others never have a chance to – simply because I practise what I preach.

Visioning or imagining the future one desires has been called creative visualization, the power of prayer and many other titles. There has even been a trend, particularly in the US, to create almost pseudo-scientific copyrighted titles for methods and techniques that are basically natural and part of how the brain works. Perhaps I should state here that I am one of those who does commit to the belief in the power of prayer and I am at ease with that kind of explanation and understanding. Nevertheless I, like a number of others who have attempted to explain this over the past century, prefer to use the associations with computing, the brain being the bio-computer. I like to use the term programming.

Our dominant thoughts tend to become our realities. Our dominant thoughts become programmes for the bio-computer. The computer runs them and through the power of the subconscious mind searches out to match up experience with the programme in the brain. By coincidence people, places and opportunities seem to appear on the horizon as we journey towards the programmed outcome. Remember my earlier statement that 96 per cent spend their entire lives helping the other 4 per cent achieve their goals?

As recently as the end of January 1994 the *Sunday Times* had a psychology feature on the findings of Dr Jacobo Grinberg, a neuro-psychologist at the National University of Mexico. His research 'suggests hidden depths in the way two minds can link together. Brain waves can synchronize without their owners realizing it.' Grinberg found that subjects who were deeply in love with each other, for example, recorded brain patterns with 'amazing similarity', and apparently he found that this similarity did not diminish even if the couple were some distance apart. The article also quotes Dr Peter Fenwick, a consultant neuro-psychologist and senior lecturer at the Institute of Psychiatry in London: 'We know we can cause unhappiness to others through our actions – that is accepted within our culture, but if mind in some way transcends brain and thinking can affect another person directly it becomes much more important that we also take responsibility for our own thoughts.'

It hasn't been easy to find pure scientific evidence and theory for what this is all about simply because mainstream science hasn't really invested into research in the field of the mind. Back at the end of the 1980s then-US President George Bush claimed that the 1990s would be 'the decade of the brain' as more and more research would be undertaken by the neuro-scientists. Hopefully more and more investment in this area will bring about more and more understanding. James Watson, who co-discovered the double helix of DNA, is quoted in a US Academy of Science book *Discovering the Brain* as saying that the brain is 'the most complex thing we have yet discovered in our Universe'. What will the final frontier and its 100 billion cells or neurons, each with its 1,000 fine tendrils reaching out to contact another, release to us in inner knowledge? I feel that science will in effect 'catch up' and explain it all for us in due course. What does seem to add up is that it all seems to work. A goal is set, the image is clear, the brainwave activity is triggered at relaxed levels and the programme is set up. Others are attracted to play their part and in time meet up and contribute. As Napoleon Hill stated in his book *Think and Grow Rich*, first published in 1933, 'What the mind can conceive and believe the mind can achieve.'

As I often say, thoughts are things. As yet we have only emerging evidence of electrical activity matching in empathic brains, but as I see it what we tend to think about constantly manifests in our lives. This can be negativity or the positive outcomes of the goal-orientated thinker. In any case, just look around you wherever you are and realize that nothing can exist before it is first of all a thought in someone's mind. Thought first – physical reality later. The right brain imagines it and left thinks out how it can be brought to reality, and usually produces it through trial and error.

Getting back to my attitude to goal-setting: it is vital and necessary if we are to move forward and solve the problems that exist in all our lives. My emphasis has to be on the vision first and the planning later, as we go. As I presently travel around the country on my busy schedule teaching MindStore, either in-house in the corporate world or on the open programmes (52 two-day programmes in 1993), I read magazines such as in-flight publications and countless others. British Midlands' in-flight offering in September 1993 featured Andrew Cohen of Betterware, who has achieved extremely impressive results. He took over the business in 1983 from the receivers for £255 thousand; 10 years later it is capitalized at £250 million. As I tend to expect from a true success, there is an apparent balance to Cohen's Wheel of Life: a passionate commitment to his business but 'family first, business second', he also looks after himself through exercise and has a number of pastimes that mean a lot to him.

The article gives four important steps he claims are fundamental to his business success. Number 1 is a clear vision: 'First we have to know where we are going.' He also has a three-year plan which he updates monthly. The plan is important but the vision comes first, and from what you can glean

119

from the article he has big visions. Belief is so important and I will return to this as we move on.

Clearly I am saying you must set goals, and if you do it in a manner that will best ensure that everything is most suited to focusing all your energy and effort on achieving it, then achieve it you must. Our MindStore methods obviously do work or there wouldn't have been the great demand for courses on them up and down the country, and I wouldn't have been successful in pursuing my own goals if I didn't practise what I preach.

Mohammed Ali was recently in Glasgow promoting his new autobiography, which is a great read. Anybody who got near him for a signing were in awe of the energy surrounding him; he had a presence that could not be missed, an outstanding man and one who has impressed millions around the world – and especially me!

In my teenage years I was particularly interested in him. I remember my father as we watched him being interviewed on television by Parkinson, pointing out how he said 'I am the greatest.' I am sure you also remember this. His absolute belief in the certainty of it was obvious, he of course said this right from the beginning as far back as I can remember. Notice he never said 'One day I will be the greatest' but 'I am, *NOW*.' This famous affirmation means so much to me and my approach to goal-setting.

You will hear so many people talk about their dreams and aspirations in future tense language. 'One day I will...have, or do, or be', but Ali talked in the present tense even before he was the greatest. Whoopi Goldberg's 'I dreamt about it all my life' implies a present tense experience of imagining the event. This is vital, to tell the subconscious constantly that you have your goal now will upset it and cause it to get to work to bring about the reality you are telling it already exists.

The great man has also shared how he actually thought out his great conquests in the ring. He has described how after agreeing to and signing a contract to fight an opponent he would settle down and imagine he was in the future. He would concentrate his mind on imagining actually being there in the ring on the night in whatever stadium and city. He would imagine that the fight had just ended. He would be standing there, once again victorious. He had just won the fight. He would focus his thinking deliberately so as to imagine how every sense in his body would be taking in the information at that time. He recorded every sense as though he were really there in that moment. Once he had done this with absolute clarity and specificity, he'd created a 'Future History'.

His 'Future History' involved what he expected to see, smell, feel, hear and taste, in full detail. Once he had experienced it as though he were actually there in the future it was history because he had lived it. He would add power to this programme by constantly reviewing it and, any time the fight entered into his thoughts, he immediately brought into his mind's eye the recorded history in the future in all its detail. Please note he never sabotaged the programme or short-circuited it by entertaining thoughts of doubt or 'I might lose.' His commitment was made, and whatever had to be done in preparation he would do.

Apart from the fact that I idolized him when I was a teenager I love his term 'Future History' and I use it on all my courses. Our target is to set powerful Future Histories in our brains that become programmes to our bio-computer. By making commitment to the programme and not being too concerned with the 'How?', we will trigger off a force or energy that will take us to our desired destinations, provided we do not sabotage it by entertaining any self-doubt.

Before we look at the MindStore technique and yet another inner room to our House on the Right Bank, let's just look once more at why I am passionate about thinking this way and resisting the need to plan it all out in advance.

When you entertain the HOW question and engage in the logic of planning it all out, the goal will be brought nearer to the current reality and present Comfort Zones. This will happen simply by exercising the left-brain faculties concerned with asking 'How?' This will demand going into the 'luggage of life' and going by past experience to determine what can be achieved and what resources are currently available. This will cause the left brain to force the goal into the realistic and achievable zone. You see, the left brain cannot know in advance how a goal will be achieved if the goal is well out of the realistic and achievable zone, in other words, if it is beyond what is currently perceived as possible.

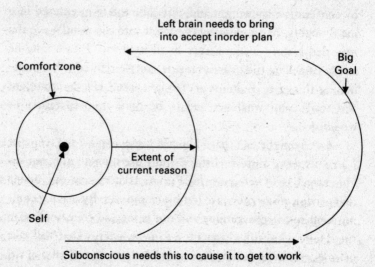

Left brain needs to bring
into accept inorder plan

Big
Goal

Comfort zone

Extent of
current reason

Self

Subconscious needs this to cause it to get to work

So, before we go any further, think BIG Future Histories – don't worry about HOW? at this stage – all will be revealed.

Remember, Einstein said: *'Imagination is more important than knowledge.'* He also said *'The things that count cannot be counted and the things that can be counted do not.'* – Fantastic.

Gestalt

Some have attempted to explain the power of programming as the process know as *Gestalt*. This is a German word meaning shape, pattern or structure. Once a pattern is set up, then should our world not match this subconscious view it will get to work and do all in its power to restore everything back to order, back to the pattern expected. For example, you can look up at a cloud on a summer's day. The cloud itself is an ever-changing mass of gas, it has no order or pattern, so to make sense of it at a deeper level you will more often than not begin to notice a shape in the cloud, perhaps it begins to look like a face, or a dog or something else. By doing this you create order for the subconscious mind.

You will have noticed something similar with wallpaper, curtain designs, patterns on the veneer of wooden furniture, etc. Similarly you might remember as a child looking up to see the man in the moon.

To highlight this phenomenon, this desire to bring back order, I have often on the second day of an in-house pro-gramme placed at random, on the wall or the curtains behind me, a torn piece of paper. This will be stuck up with blue tack or sellotape and will be set off to the side of where I would normally stand and teach. Almost immediately on settling down the class will begin to notice it, indeed they spend a lot of time

123

being distracted by it. Their eyes regularly move off me and on to the now annoying interruption that just shouldn't be there. It is absolutely amazing how often someone at the first rest period gets up and takes it down, and of course immediately sighs from relief and starts to feel good again. They have got things back to normal and in order.

Well, if we constantly use self-talk, like Mohammed Ali did, with positive, present tense affirmations, or review specific images in our minds of Future Histories like Whoopi Goldberg, did then Gestalt will take place and the subconscious once again will get to work to bring about order. Since the present reality doesn't match, the subconscious has to find people, places and opportunities and provide the inner drive that causes you to take the action you must take to bring it about. Fantastic! However it works – let me tell you *'It Only Works!'*

How then can we go about setting goals? Many people, on first approaching goal-setting, actually find it difficult to think about what their goals should be. If you are like this yourself then do not be too concerned. Join the vast majority – remember it's probably true that only 4 per cent do it anyway. I believe your starting point should be your Wheel of Life. Begin there and decide to set your goals according to which sections of your Wheel obviously need attention.

Remember, our focus is on the positive. Goals are all about what you want to be, do and have – not what you don't want to be, do or have.

Now, do not concern yourself with 'What if I set the wrong goal?' There is no right or wrong with this. The task is to get started with any goal – you can have more than one but my advice is not to have too many – learn to walk before you run, but do think BIG on the outcome. As I explain the technique, do not at this time concern yourself with the time-scale, I will

124

cover this important point in Chapter 9.

Once you are up and running, meaningful goals and desires that really get you motivated will emerge anyway; it's the journey that counts more than the destination as you will soon find out.

The Four Steps of Goal-setting

There is a logic to goal-setting that is worth pointing out since our approach inevitably involves using both brains. Let's look at the left-brain approach before examining the right-brained MindStore technique. The starting point will be the presence of a problem – for most people the problem will be just not having a goal – but just say a situation exists that you want to change or improve on. There are four key steps:

> Problem
> 1. Admit and accept you have a problem

- First of all may I say that the positive thinker doesn't use the word problem anyway, preferring the words challenge or opportunity. Such language has specific and positive direction-orientated meaning to the brain, whereas 'problem' means stuck in the present negative limiting position. So with Delete that Programme take the word 'problem' out of your vocabulary, as I have done.

- You will tend to find that most people are 'problem'-orientated in their thinking, very rarely solution-orientated. They can describe the 'problem' in great detail and may

125

spend hours in their thinking, actually reflecting on it in all its meaning and importance. In our office the MindStore team are encouraged not to bring to meetings 'problems' but 'solutions', possible ways forward, and if they are stuck then we do indeed have a challenge.

- This first stage of admitting that a 'problem' does exist is a challenge in itself. Most people find this could be a lot easier. Much of our desire is to want to blame someone else, to point a finger outwards rather than accept responsibility oneself. Many problems can be continuously swept under the carpet because of a sense of shame or guilt at having one in the first case.

- As I have said before, I used to think that success was actually reaching a point in life when problems just didn't exist any more. Images of desert islands and a life of luxury in sunny climes were forever present. The truth is that to be alive is to have problems. So let's begin to admit they do exist in our lives, because let's face it everyone has them, yours just happen to be different from everyone else's. Yours are yours and theirs are theirs.

- The sense of guilt that many people experience when admitting they have a problem goes back to childhood, I'd suggest. The ensuing row, punishment or embarrassment when you admitted to doing something 'naughty' has probably taught you that admitting is painful. And since we don't actually move towards pain through choice, opting instead to move away from it and back to comfort, most of us find it challenging to actually admit any problem.

- How about this: next time you discover a problem exists in your life and you want to point the finger of blame at something or someone else, remember:

- One finger points out, one points up above and three point right back to yourself. Our positive 'Fantastic' approach is that there must be a good reason for this challenge. You can grow and develop from this, that's why one finger points to heaven. Three point right to you yourself, because the problem is yours.

- Accept a challenge but decide to solve it and put it right, move towards finding a solution. Love yourself enough to accept that you are only human and that since to be alive is to have challenges to overcome, feel good and grasp the opportunity to live to the full.

```
                    Problem
    1. Admit and accept you have a problem
                  2. Analyse it
```

- Analyse your problem. Make sure, be specific about who is involved, when it happens, where it happens, why it happens and how it occurs. Focus fully on the whole problem, warts and all. Do not falling into the trap of only addressing what you are comfortable with. If it is painful we have a technique built into the MindStore way that will ease this for you.

```
                    Problem
    1. Admit and accept you have a problem
                  2. Analyse it
              3. Look for an alternative
```

- We are now moving away from the problem and into the solution. Begin to explore alternative behaviour, situations or actions. Logic tells us that if we look at all the other options then one of them, at least, will be the solution.

```
                    Problem
    1. Admit and accept you have a problem
                  2. Analyse it
              3. Look for alternatives
          4. Focus your energy on the solution
```

- Once you select an alternative you have your solution. The focus of all thought and activity must now be on the solution and never again on the problem. At the moment you now have a goal or desired outcome and it really is as simple as that. However, if the process is just applied at the wide-awake left-brain-dominant Beta levels, then the chances are that really creative and fresh ideas and solutions will not be forthcoming. Indeed, you may find yourself stuck back at stage Two, in other words stuck with the problem. This is why an approach that will involve both brains will be of maximum benefit, and therefore this is the MindStore way.

Summary

1. 96 per cent spend their entire lives helping the other 4 per cent achieve their goals!
2. Create your own future rather than have someone else create it for you.
3. Think BIG and resist the temptation to limit your goals by asking HOW?
4. Place your emphasis on the vision and let the plan develop on your journey towards your goal.
5. Create Gestalt by constantly reviewing your Future History while ensuring that your self-talk reinforces your belief that you will achieve.
6. The four logical steps in goal-setting:

   1) Admit and accept you have a problem.
   2) Analyse it.
   3) Look for an alternative.
   4) Focus your energy on the solution.

8

The Editing Suite

Yes, this chapter deals with the construction of a new room within your House on the Right Bank. This is a very important room and one that you will use every day, if like me and thousands of others you make this a way of life.

The mental architecture this time involves a room set off the Central Hallway. We will call it the Editing Suite. It will be used for problem-solving and for creating Future Histories and goals in your life. It's a powerful room, so it's important that you make it attractive to your mind. You will again decide on the shape of the room and the height of the ceiling, the decorative features, colours and lighting.

On one of the walls you will erect the main tools. Along the top of the wall you will place what we will call a 'time frame'.

FUTURE	PRESENT	PAST

This is a narrow panel that divides the wall in three. On the panel you can place dates. The central panel is for the present date, today's date whenever you use the room. The right-hand panel as you look at it in your mind's eye is for dates in the past; the left-hand panel is for future dates. My reasoning for structuring time like this is quite simple and I will explain it below.

Next, suspended on the wall just below the time frame you will place three gigantic cinema screens. One in the middle for the now, one to the left for your Future Histories, and one to the right for your past recordings.

	DATE	
FUTURE HISTORY	NOW	PAST RECORDINGS

Facing the centre screen you will place a comfortable chair (a Director's chair) as you will now become the Director of your own Movies of Life. By the chair you will need a projector and a remote control handset for operating the screens. Before I explain how we use the Editing Suite, let's be clear about the positioning of the screens.

Since we accept that the autonomic nervous system crosses from the left side of the brain to work the right side of the body and vice versa, my thinking here is that by placing the screens in this format you will maximize your thinking as follows. The screen on the right is for your past experience, to be used to analyse a problem. Since this is a left-brain activity it seems obvious that if the eyes look to the right to do this then the left side of the brain, through the autonomic nervous system, will be engaged and therefore enhance your capacity to analyse. Likewise, by looking to the left for the future you will actually stimulate more right-brain creativity and be able to produce imagined futures and solutions.

Some of you who have studied Neurolinguistic Programming (NLP) will be aware of a contradiction here with accepted eye movements in relation to audio, kinesthetic and visual thinking. Many of you will not be and if you wish to find out more about this fascinating material I strongly recommend Anthony Robbins' best-selling book, *Unlimited Power* (particularly chapter 8). I have long recommended this book to everyone who attends my courses. I actually believe that if you combine MindStore with Robbins' work then you would have a tremendous edge or advantage in all you do.

NLP has established that the vast majority of people will position their eyes in particular places when using different types of thought. This can be observed when someone is receiving visual, emotional or auditory input. I choose not to cover this in detail but since many readers may be aware of NLP I didn't want to confuse them. When someone is engaged in remembering a visual image they tend to lift their eyes up and to the left. This directly contradicts my placing of the cinema screens in the Editing Suite. My response is very simple and not too scientific. These positions are noticed when the eyes are open and when presumably higher brainwave activity is generated. Our technique is used with the eyes closed at lower frequencies, and in our Editing Suite screen we will be using all the senses to experience not just visual stimuli but also sound, feelings, taste, etc.

I have added this little point just so that those who are enthusiasts for NLP do not miss out on the powerful effects of the Editing Suite. Who knows, one day research may provide us with a deeper understanding of why the screens work, but let me assure you they *only work* – as you will find out.

Programming Your Future History

The MindStore technique, then, is as follows. Whenever you have a challenge and you seek to solve it or wish to set a goal, then take some space, sit down and relax. You will find that high Beta frequency and uptight worrying provide little in the way of ideas and can be of no personal benefit. Enter your House on the Right Bank by the Standard Entry Exercise. Remember, solutions and creativity naturally spring forth when we are relaxed and away from the humdrum of daily life.

Have an imagined shower in your Conditioning Gym and enter your Editing Suite by the Central Hallway. Once there, it is a good idea to remind yourself of its layout: the three screens, the time frame, the Director's chair, the projector and the remote control handset. Sit in your Director's chair and, with the remote control, pretend to project onto the central screen your current situation or challenge. Your motive here is to admit and accept that it does exist. You may find in doing this that you could find it easier to do, perhaps you do wish to blame someone else or you find negative emotions welling up from within. You will find it useful to take the remote control and just turn down the intensity of the senses projected on the screen. For example, you can make the scene smaller and push it away from you into the distance. This will

134

give you a feeling of control and will make the image no longer such a threat; you will now be better able to admit and accept it. Likewise, sounds, feelings and especially emotions can be 'adjusted' in this way.

You can project into your past on the right-hand screen to make a more intensive study of the situation, e.g. recent manifestations of the challenge, where it has happened before, whom it involved, when, etc. The idea is to be honest with yourself at this point and you will certainly find it easier to do if you are. Often you will gain fresh insights and new perspectives on the issues you examine. Once you feel you have focused your mind and can admit and accept the current reality, then you can move back to the central screen.

Once again, project your current status on the central screen but now take your remote control and turn down all senses until it all becomes a distant dot on the central screen. At this point press an imagined delete button on your control and the dot disappears. Now you no longer have the challenge, you have just erased the programme from the bio-computer.

Project now to the left-hand screen and allow your mind to create and explore Future Histories, i.e. solutions. Once you have settled on the outcome you desire, then in order to build the strength of the imagined future or goal you deliberately and fully establish this new programme in your brain by doing just what Mohammed Ali did. Specifically ask yourself what you expect to see when you achieve your goal. You will find by intensifying the image – making the scene bigger and bringing it nearer – that you will be more able to associate with the image. Make it brighter and freeze-frame the image in brilliant white light. Do the same with the other senses, and be deliberate – what do you expect to hear? Particularly, how will you feel? Focus on the emotions that success will produce in this case.

You will now have a Future History, but like Mohammed Ali you have to give it power in order to bring about the necessary Gestalt in your brain. Reinforce the image, sounds and feelings by regularly reminding yourself of your programme. It is important that once you have your Future History in place that's all you think about in the future. You only look to your future screen on the left, never ever go back over the central or past (right-hand) screens.

In effect you will be 'grooving' into your mind, just as grooves are pressed onto a vinyl record, the outcome you have established in a future reality. Programming or grooving works, the Gestalt will soon be established and, as Goethe implied, all manner of events will unfold till you achieve your end. People, places and opportunities will be attracted into your life as if by coincidence.

You must be specific with your outcome because this does *only work*, so be careful in your detail. I remember years ago sitting down and programming that I was working at Parkhead, the home of my favourite football club Celtic. I have been a lifelong fan and my dream was to teach them these techniques and to become involved with the players and management. Might I point out here that although I have worked extensively and at the highest level in many sports, back then I hadn't and this was an 'unrealistic' and 'unachievable' type of goal I can assure you.

My programming on the Future Screen produced images of the changing rooms and the tunnel and dug-out and all the excitement of the big match day. I must tell you that I simply took for granted that since this was at Parkhead that the Celtic team were involved; I didn't focus my mind and specifically see them and hear them in the future screen image. Well some years later I made it, I arrived with the team bus, we got the gear into the dressing room, the players and myself walked out pre-match onto the hallowed turf, we sat in the dug-out and returned to the dressing room as the crowd began to filter in.

The pre-match talk by the manager was complete and the players and I then got down to programming a successful match. At five minutes to three the referee came in and inspected the players' boots before the captains led out the teams to a thunderous roar from the crowd. At last my programme had come true (just as they do), I was at Parkhead for a Celtic match – *BUT* I was with Dundee United!

You must be specific with your programming – *'It Only Works!'*

The brain prefers a specific goal in fine detail so that it can get to work to identify what is required to bring it about. You will find anyway that by being specific and by defining the outcome well you will be able to picture the goal better. Your subconscious needs a vivid visual image in order to impact it. You will find that intense emotional feelings will help to hold your attention on your Future History.

Remember, the correct approach here is to think BIG and not to be too concerned about how you are going to achieve your goal. The energy at this point has to be focused on convincing the subconscious that the Future History has already occurred.

Let me tell you another story from my experience of working in sport. One day in 1988 I sat at home with my wife Norma and we watched on television the final of the women's 10,000-metre race at the Seoul Olympics. As a Brit and especially as a Scot I was willing Liz McColgan on to win. We were shouting at the screen and becoming more and more excited as Liz was way out in front lap after lap. She was surely going to win the

Gold medal – it was fantastic.

Eventually a Russian girl seemed to emerge from the pack and started to get nearer and nearer to Liz. Finally in the last bend they were neck and neck. They both were giving their all, but alas Bonderenko edged in front and ran away to cross the line first. Liz came in a really disappointed second – winning a Silver Medal was a great achievement but Liz seemed devastated.

To cut a long story short, Liz was interviewed by the BBC at the trackside monitor, they re-ran the video of the final lap with the Russian bearing down on her and there on screen you could see Liz looking back over her shoulder. The interviewer noticed this and asked her what she was doing. Liz told the world that she actually felt that if the Russian got in front of her she would lose. In that final and crucial bend Liz explained how she did all she could to find the final spurt of energy so as to kick out for the tape but she just couldn't find it.

I will never forget that moment – I am passionate about thought producing reality – and I turned to Norma and actually said there and then 'I've got to get Liz McColgan.' We both sat there and closed our eyes and programmed my teaching her in the privacy of her own home. Remember, 'It Only Works.' Almost a year to the day later I was teaching at a branch of a life insurance company in Dundee when one of the participants took me aside and said that he knew of someone who could do with this type of approach, and that if I wished he would attempt to set up a meeting.

To my absolute joy, this man, Iain, was a very good friend of Liz and Pete McColgan. A week later there I was in her home and a good friendship began. Liz and Pete are among the nicest people you could ever meet and her commitment to what she does is second to none. Indeed she is a model in my mind for determination and, when she won the World Championship medal in Tokyo in a race many believe to be the finest feat in athletic history, it was a humbling experience to know that I had met her on the way.

You see it does *only work*, do not concern yourself with how – but rather make your commitment to your vision. You can and must use the screens to programme for everything and anything. You know everybody is programming all the time anyway. The person who gets up on a wet and windy morning, gets caught in a traffic jam before getting to work and says to him- or herself 'I bet it's going to be one of those days' is programming a negative day. Indeed the subconscious will be forced to focus the conscious mind on what apparently goes wrong, and of course this person will fail to see any of the positive input that in truth is all around.

I programme everything, for example as I write this it is a Saturday morning. In the afternoon I plan to take my sons, along with their grandfather, to an exhibition in the city. We are all looking forward to it so the programme is running anyway. Tonight Norma and I have a table booked at one of Glasgow's finest restaurants. What you can be sure of is that we both won't just turn up and take our places. We will both visit our Editing Suites and programme a fantastic evening on our future screens.

I programme everything, and you know what? I just keep getting the outcomes I desire in my life. And if the programme doesn't work out, as occasionally it doesn't, then my attitude is 'Fantastic; there must be a good reason for this' and I simply accept it and move on. Think about it. How often in your life has an event occurred that you were really disappointed about? Perhaps you believed it to be a major setback, maybe you didn't get a job or failed to reach some necessary standard or whatever.

139

Only now you look back and realize that something better occurred later and indeed the apparent disappointment was actually the best thing that could have happened.

Now, since we do not concern ourselves with HOW within the Editing Suite but rather on the clarity of the outcome itself it is vital that we have the correct attitude to the programme.

Desire, Belief and Certainty

There are no limitations to the mind except those we acknowledge.

NAPOLEON HILL

Once you get into programming and you see the results you will soon recognize Napoleon Hill's great truth: we are limited only by our own thoughts. Again this is why we must think BIG when it comes to setting our goals. The first requirement, though, is that you must have a massive DESIRE for your outcome. Nothing will happen if the DESIRE is not there, since it is the source of energy that lifts you up and gets you towards your the goal. The DESIRE is what overcomes procrastination, it is necessary to break inertia and is vital for building the momentum required.

The bigger your DESIRE to achieve your goal then the more likely you are to achieve it. You really need to want whatever it is in your life. You will find you can build a strong DESIRE by actually focusing your mind on the benefits that will come your way as you achieve your goal. I strongly advise writing the benefits down; you can find them by thinking about the reasons why you want a particular outcome in your life. Incidentally, constantly reviewing your Future History on the left-hand screen will build the inner strength of your DESIRE, especially if you have been specific in detail about your goal.

Anyone who has achieved knows that disappointment, setbacks and hurdles are met on the journey; at times it feels like it would be easier to give up. But if the goal is worth having then it is worth paying the price. At times when you doubt yourself and your belief is low, DESIRE will keep you going. If you don't really desire the goal you set, then to put it simply you don't have one. Everyone I have met who has achieved undoubtedly wanted to achieve their goal more than anything else.

Once the inertia is gone and you start to build your momentum towards the goal, you need a second element in order to bring about your success. You need to BELIEVE that you can and will achieve. You build this vital aspect again by reviewing your Future History. In doing so your subconscious will adjust your Comfort Zone to a higher level. Once the new level is established you cannot fail to have a deep inner BELIEF that the outcome is yours. You can focus your mind on BELIEF by writing down why you deserve the goal you have set.

Finally you have to have a sense of CERTAINTY that it will occur. You simply know and indeed expect it to happen. You know it's on its way provided you do whatever has to be done on the journey with a sense of absolute CERTAINTY. In your programming remember to focus in on the Future screen but as though it is happening now, to build CER-TAINTY you need to decide to accept the outcome as you view it on the left-hand screen, to claim it unconditionally as yours.

If a goal is not achieved then you can usually check back on the above three (DESIRE, BELIEF and CERTAINTY), or indeed if someone gives up before the journey is in real swing then again one or more of these three elements is not what it should be or even missing. I recommend constantly checking your DESIRE, BELIEF and CERTAINTY to check that you are on target. If one of these three needs a bit of energy to push it up then focus your mind on it. Review your benefits in the case of DESIRE, check your sense of deservedness with BELIEF, and be CERTAIN that you have accepted your goals as belonging to you in your future present tense programming.

Now as you might expect I have a full system that will ensure that all the correct steps are taken, but let me just give you a word of warning: *Be very careful about keeping your goals to yourself.* Never share your goals with anybody else unless you are sure they will support you in it, that they will wish you well and genuinely be happy for you in your achievement. This is vital because many a dream has had the energy and drive taken out of it by loved ones, friends or colleagues who didn't understand the truth of what we have shared in these pages.

Remember they also have their Comfort Zones, even Comfort Zones about their relationship with you. If you explain to them what you intend to do, be or have, and especially since it will be a BIG goal, then they of course will be unable to see it. They may laugh or get upset, they may feel that they will lose the one they presently love or value or they may even resent any idea of you rising 'above your station'. Your own subconscious, especially in the beginning, would prefer that you didn't use your Editing Suite because it knows that it works – indeed, *'It Only Works.'* It would rather keep the world the way it is now, even if that is the most negative of present realities. But it will have to get to work.

Your friends or loved ones don't want you to succeed because deep down they actually know that they can change too but they don't really want to. If you change then they may have to confront this great truth – and what if they do not join you in growing, how will they feel?

Be careful about all of this. The most loving and caring way to assist them is for you to get on with your own progress. They will notice the change towards positivity. They will admire your newfound energy and enthusiasm. These are attracting forces that will cause them to become curious about what you are doing. Over time they will see that you are well on your way and doing better, and the chances are they will want to get involved themselves and grow too.

A vision is something no one else can see.

ANITA RODDICK

Let's get into the House on the Right Bank and construct this wonderful room – your Editing Suite – before we take a closer look (in the next chapter) at how you can use it to fantastic effect in all areas of your life.

EXERCISE 5: THE EDITING SUITE
Find a comfortable position in your chair, close your eyes and begin breathing in a regular and slow manner. We will now begin to focus your mind and body on relaxing into a healthy state of being. Once again, as I mention each part of your body concentrate on it and focus your thinking on producing relaxation.

Take a deep breath and relax...take another deep breath and relax...take a deep breath and again relax...

My scalp is relaxed, I feel my scalp relaxed... My

forehead is relaxed, I feel my forehead relaxed... My eyelids are relaxed, I feel my eyelids relaxed... My face is relaxed, I feel my face relaxed... My tongue is relaxed, I feel my tongue relaxed... My jaw is relaxed, I feel my jaw relaxed... My throat is relaxed, I feel my throat relaxed...

My shoulders are relaxed, I feel my shoulders relaxed... My arms and hands are relaxed, I feel my arms and hands relaxed... My upper back is relaxed, I feel my upper back relaxed... My chest is relaxed, I feel my chest relaxed... My lower back is relaxed, I feel my lower back relaxed...

My abdomen is relaxed, I feel my abdomen relaxed... My hips are relaxed, I feel my hips relaxed... My thighs are relaxed, I feel my thighs relaxed... My knees are relaxed, I feel my knees relaxed... My calves are relaxed, I feel my calves relaxed... My ankles are relaxed, I feel my ankles relaxed... My toes are relaxed, I feel my toes relaxed... My soles are relaxed, I feel my soles relaxed... My heels are relaxed, I feel my heels relaxed...

Take a deep breath and relax...

I will now imagine that I am in a very special place of relaxation... I fully pretend that I am there...I will give myself a short period to engage fully in this and enjoy it [30 seconds]...

Take a deep breath and relax... I will now adjust and

imagine that I am standing on the river bank, the river is behind me and I am facing into a wonderful landscape...

I can feel my feet on the lush green grass...overhead the sky is deep blue and the air is fresh with the scent of the meadow...I can hear the sounds of the wonderful landscape before me...

I now move forward and through the doorway of my house with the red roof...into my Entrance Vestibule, past my Symbol of Potential and on into my Conditioning Gym...

In a moment I will stand within my shower and cleanse away any current negativity...

I now enter my showering area and turn on the flow in order that its imaginary cleansing action can commence...I pretend to feel the warm spring waters run through my hair and down over every inch of my body, draining away mental fatigue and restoring vibrant life in its wake...

I now imagine the bright sunlight reaching deep within, filtering out and washing away all my limiting and destructive attitudes, particularly my negative thinking today...

Readjusting and turning off the shower I now step out, instantly dried and fresh with positive expectations...

In a moment I will create my Editing Suite, which is entered by a doorway off my Central Hallway... It will be used for problem-solving and goal-setting...

I now leave my Conditioning Gym and enter my Central Hallway, the walls covered with images depicting times from my past when I have been at my very best... I now create the room that will house my Editing Suite... I decide on its shape the height of the ceiling...now the decorative features, colours and lighting... On one of the walls, high up near the ceiling I will place a time-frame for programming dates... Suspended on the wall just below the time-frame I now erect three gigantic cinema screens: One in the middle for the now, one to the left for my Future Histories, and one to the right for my past recordings...

Facing the central screen I will now install a Director's chair... Now a projector and remote control handset for operating the screens... I will project images onto the screens for the purpose of setting goals and problem-solving...

In future I will admit and accept that I have a challenge that I wish to change by projecting its current situation on the central screen... I can go into the past screen on the right to analyse... By using my remote control I can return to the central screen and turn down the image, feelings and sounds until it becomes an instant dot... I can then imagine pressing a delete button to remove the programme completely from the screen... Now on the left-hand (future) screen

I will explore alternatives before selecting the one I truly want for my life at this time... I will make it bigger and bigger, bringing it closer to me before freeze-framing it in brilliant white light... I will then have a Future History...

Regularly reviewing my Future Histories on the left-hand screen will build my Desire, Belief and Certainty that I will achieve my goal or desired outcome...

I have now created my Editing Suite... I will use it for attracting into my life the people, places and opportunities I need to achieve my goals...

I will now leave my house and return to the river's edge... I feel the lush green grass beneath my feet... I will shortly count from 1 to 7 and gradually adjust to come out of this healthy state of deep relaxation... 1...2...3...4...now beyond the midpoint, when I open my eyes I will be wide awake and revitalized both physically and mentally...5, I begin to adjust my body...6, I prepare to open my eyes...and 7, I open my eyes, wide awake now, both physically and mentally alert.

Summary

1. The Central Screen is for the now, the Left-hand Screen for your Future Histories, and the Right-hand Screen is

for your past recordings.

2. Make sure that your Future Histories are programmed with specific detail.

3. Once a programme is set up never review your past recordings but focus only on the Future History.

4. Get into the habit of programming everything that matters. Take Quality Recovery Time and mentally rehearse on your Future Screen the outcomes you desire.

5. Commit yourself to developing strong Desire, Belief and Certainty for your outcomes.

6. Be careful in sharing your goals with others, be sensitive of their Comfort Zones and expectations.

9

Programming Your Day/ The Night Book

The MindStore techniques do *only work*, but remember you will tend to stay within current Comfort Zones and your subconscious doesn't really want you to change. The chances are that even though you sense that by using these techniques you will succeed, you may also realize that you yourself may well procrastinate and put things off. It is often said that the most challenging part on the road to achieving a goal is actually setting it and taking the first step. The final step is easy and the journey in between is exciting, but you do have to begin.

The discipline of reviewing your Future History is vital if you are to achieve your goal. In reality, though, it is actually quite easy: all you have to do is make your commitment. Then again, the commitment thing is the hardest part. I am convinced that once you set your commitment to the goal, you're there, it's just a matter of time.

Over the years that I have been teaching this I have inevitably met many people who have attended a course with me some time before. I always ask them how they are doing and if I get the 'natural' response of 'Not too bad, thanks' I know immediately that they are not practising and have missed the point of the MindStore way. What will be true, though, is that they will not even notice the language they have just used, and in fact they will enthuse about how the techniques work for them. This 'success' will usually be on easy and immediate programming results, such as getting parking places in busy towns or the best table in a popular restaurant, having a good night out or doing well at the occasional important meeting. But they are not applying it to the bigger, more powerful areas of their lives and gaining success there.

I am not knocking this because whether they like it or not or will accept it or not they are up against the Comfort Zone challenge. My belief is that we do fear success and resist change. Such people have long since given up on real growth and are content to know they have these powerful techniques and can use them for instant results and gratification.

You might appreciate that over the years I have become quite frustrated with encountering this type of response. Of course many, many people have and do use the techniques for massive change and succeed in doing so, but all of us can achieve much, much more. So I have set about working out a day-to-day routine that ensures that the Gestalt takes place and that the programmes most definitely run. It has taken me some time but I believe I now have the ultimate system to ensure that you get the results you are looking for. However, it does require a little discipline.

The MindStore way has two important elements: Programming your Day, and the Night Book. Let's look at programming your day first, it will serve as the fuel to drive you forward. The Night Book, which we'll discuss later, will be your vehicle.

Once you understand that all this does work and you have made it a way of life you, like me, will find that you just cannot imagine ever going into your day without first programming it. Programming becomes like brushing your teeth and combing your hair – you just have to do it or you don't feel right. What is really exciting is that programming your day will impact and last right throughout your day.

Programming Your Day

So, every single morning begin by waking about 15 minutes earlier than usual. Make this an established pattern. The technique you will learn in the next chapter will assist you to do this easily. I recommend rising and relieving yourself before returning to your bed to sit up and, in a warm and comfortable position, enter your House on the Right Bank, have a shower and go immediately to your Editing Suite. Always remind yourself of its layout, this will serve as a trigger to alert your subconscious that you are about to programme. Your subconscious will thus adjust and pay attention to what follows.

On your central screen project an image of your diary for the day. Focus your mind and chronologically run through the expected schedule. Be sure to include any social activity or evening commitments with family or friends. For example:

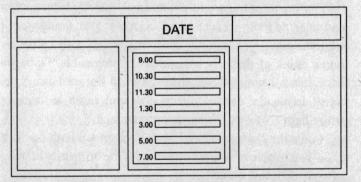

Bring up a diary page for your day ahead on the central screen.

Then take the first event of the day, whatever it is, and look to your right-hand (past) screen and there relive the last time you were involved in the same type of activity and did it well. At this point you are recognizing that you are a successful person and of course you are energizing the part of your brain where this is stored. This will give you confidence and trigger expectations of success to come.

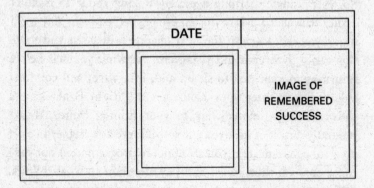

Notice how the central screen is now unfocused while all your energy is engaged in looking to the right-hand screen and remembering the previous success.

Now the most important phase. Look into the future screen and imagine today's event going exactly as you would want it to. Remember, you will not concern yourself with HOW but rather think of the very best outcome imaginable. Once you have, like Mohammed Ali, created a vivid Future History you freeze-frame the desired outcome or end result in brilliant, white light. Now that event is programmed.

Notice the central and right-hand screen are both blank, to allow you to give maximum attention to the brilliantly lit image of your expected outcome.

Next you go through exactly the same process for the second, third, etc. events in your day until your entire day is programmed.

This may take 10 to 15 minutes to do first thing in the morning, but it is invaluable. In this way you actually start your day by taking some Quality Recovery Time even before

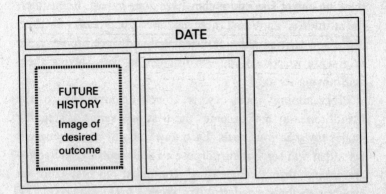

you begin. You also set up patterns of powerful and positive expectations for the day ahead. Once you have completed your programming I recommend returning to your Energizing Beam in the Conditioning Gym before counting from 1 to 7 and opening your eyes, a way of celebrating in advance a truly fantastic day.

The secret here is to make this a way of life. The more you do it, the more it works. You may think that your early morning regime just won't allow for this, but remember I have asked you to wake up 15 minutes earlier to facilitate your practice of it. Still, if you feel it will disturb others then find another solution – perhaps you could do it in another room or in the privacy of your own head during your journey if you take public transport to work. If you can't control your external environment, do it when you get to work, but I can assure you that first thing in bed is the best time without question. Go on, just get on with it and observe how you tend to get the day you programme.

Occasionally, because life is like this, surprises and disappointments may appear during your day. You will find that these no longer faze you as they have done in past. Remember, the attitude is 'Fantastic; there must be a good reason for this.' Since you are now solution-orientated and since problems are in a sense welcomed you can just get on with solving them and moving forward.

Programming your day is a vital component to the MindStore way and becomes the first in a series of stepping stones towards your goals. Each day you will be carrying out tasks that will serve their purpose on your journey, so by programming them you ensure continued success and an expectation for a wonderful day ahead. *'It Only Works!'*

It will amaze you just how often people, places and opportunities just seem to be attracted into your day to ensure your programme comes about. I also recommend that as the day goes on you take vital QRT, particularly before important events of the day. Taking a full physical relaxation will dissipate the effects of stress and refocus your energy. By reviewing your Future History and mentally rehearsing on your future screen the event that is about to take place you will be able to bring all your physical and mental faculties to bear and with absolute confidence you will do your very best and achieve your desired outcome.

The Night Book

The Night Book system brings about real change. It builds self-confidence and the belief that you can and will achieve. It is a vital process to ensure that both your conscious and your subconscious are focused on where you are going. It takes a bit of time to set up as it is a major project in its own right.

You will find, however, that you fully enjoy putting it together, and once in order you will experience a tremendous sense of achievement. You will feel special because you will be one of the 4 per cent who actually writes out their goals – and in your case the detail and clarity of thought represented on paper will have a truly substantial impact.

I will now describe step by step the complete Night Book system and how to set up your own. Some of the steps are vital and some almost serve as icing on the cake – not absolutely vital but making a worthwhile difference. I can tell you that it is tried and tested and, again, *it only works*.

EQUIPMENT

You will need:

- a large loose-leaf binder (preferably lever arch file)
- blank A4-sized paper
- access to a photocopier
- a pen and ruler
- scissors
- magazines and brochures
- paper glue

What you will put together here is your own private property and I strongly urge you not to let anybody see it, unless you can be absolutely sure they will support your aspirations and wish you well in your achievements.

First buy yourself a large loose-leaf folder (preferably a lever arch file). It must be a brand new one and one you have personally invested in. You should go to the effort of purchasing it yourself. Right from the word go you are making a statement to your subconscious that *you mean business* and, since this is about your future, you ought to have no previous association with the folder you use. I recommend a lever arch file because they are usually big and tend to stand freely by themselves on the floor or on a shelf.

You can go to the extra effort of purchasing a set of dividers for the various sections of your Night Book. Coloured paper for each section can also add to the visual appeal of its contents. Even different coloured felt-tip pens are useful, although not vital. When it comes to making a statement of your future intent it is probably wise to represent yourself in the best possible light, and certainly a book with an air of prosperity about it and not penny-pinching meanness will be required if grand change is to occur. In any event just imagine if you did have to show it once completed to someone else; I am sure you would want to be proud of your efforts as well as what you are looking forward to.

Next arrange to get access to a photocopier and run off the various sheets outlined below. A photocopier will make it easier for you, however you can if you prefer put each page together by hand. Either way will be just fine.

SECTION 1 – THE WHEEL OF LIFE

Make up six sheets with the Wheel of Life – you will need six since I recommend plotting it every two months so as to be able to see your progress while at the same time ensuring that you are maintaining a sense of balance and not putting too much effort into just one particular area.

The Wheel of Life will allow you to sense where you need to set goals so as to bring balance into your life.

So, by plotting your Wheel you will be able to reflect on

where you are in your life at this time. You will need to make a statement of intent, and it is more than useful to begin by actually acknowledging your current strengths and achievements.

WHEEL OF LIFE

Date. . . . .

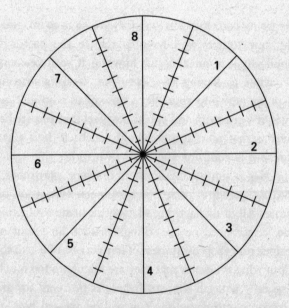

SECTION 2 – GRATIFICATION LIST

It is vital to acknowledge and 'count your blessings', you are a special person and as your Central Hallway should depict you have strengths and achievements already. I recommend giving yourself a pat on the back by writing down and listing all that you are grateful for at present. Remember it is all too easy to put yourself down, so do look closely at your situation at present and freely appreciate just who and what you are. It is important to enjoy the journey as you travel to your goals, so continue to add to the list as success begins to manifest and you move forward.

A couple of pages is usually enough here.

SECTION 3 – ELIMINATION LIST

In preparing your mind to look forward so as to imagine freely bright new futures you have to release the past with joy. Symbolically it is amazing just how much positive energy you can generate by having a big clear-out, creating space quickly attracts the new into your life. Those of us who do this really enjoy it, it's great fun and you almost feel that you are breaking the chains that bind you and hold you back. It is a symbolic gesture but is good for you in its own right.

The idea is simple: clean out all drawers, wardrobes, desks, cupboards, garages, lofts, filing cabinets, even your bag and briefcase. All of us have stored away all manner of things that we no longer need or use, things that no longer fit or have long since past their usefulness. They may be of use to someone else, but what is clear is that they are taking up too much room and space – with all this stuff there is no room for anything else to come into your life. You will be amazed how quickly, once emptied of the old, how the drawers, wardrobes, cupboards, etc. become filled again, but this time with the new.

This in itself does become quite fascinating and you can really go to town. You can give lots away to charity, even expensive items that no longer fit or that you know you just won't use again. You can easily take them all off to a car boot sale and have fun, but make sure you don't swap it all for someone else's rubbish – that serves no real purpose to you. Accept that all this clutter blocks up your readiness to receive your future benefits. It's almost crazy but it does work, so get busy: write out your list of what must go, and act on it.

Again a couple of pages is more than enough here. Be sure to release and forgive family, friends, colleagues and neighbours here too. Holding on to resentment for someone else is a powerful energy that of course works in the opposite direction to that in which you wish to journey. Resentments bind you to the past with chains of steel, so list these too and decide to forgive and release the negative energy and open up to a bright new and exciting future.

SECTION 4 – FINDING YOUR GOAL – THE FIRST STAGE

With the MindStore approach of emphasizing the vision and not asking HOW too early we are also aware that the 'luggage of life' will have its impact and may, no matter how big you choose to think, hold you back especially as a beginner. So I recommend setting goals that initially only concern yourself, with a time-scale of up to 12 months. Many people will want to set long-term goals, indeed you will want to dream of futures that logic will tell you will take much longer than 12 months to achieve, but do explore my thinking here a little bit further.

You see, if you look to, say, three years' hence and set a goal, then your 'luggage of life' will put its oar in. If, however, you do think big for the next 12 months you will find that one year from now, still thinking big, you can set and achieve even more in year two. By the time you are looking out to the third year you will set standards of expectation way beyond what

159

you could have imagined two years before. Once you are convinced by our approach then you can truly go for it and set your longer-term outlooks. Of course, it's up to you. If need be then do set them for as far in the future as you wish.

Fill in the following sheet without concerning yourself about what's possible or how you are going to achieve it. Just ask yourself, 'What do I want?' This will help to focus your mind. If you find that you seem stuck and are unable to find suitable ideas, then enter your Editing Suite and explore possibilities with your Future Screen. Think in terms of what you want to be or have or do in each section of your Wheel of Life between now and three months from now (short term), and now and 1 year from now (long term).

SECTION	SHORT TERM	LONG TERM
FAMILY		
SOCIAL		
PERSONAL DEVELOPMENT		
HEALTH		
ATTITUDE		
CAREER		
FINANCIAL		
SPIRITUAL		

This serves as a starting point. All you need is rough ideas at this stage. The exact and specific working required to make your goal work for you will come in a later phase.

You can have one long- and one short-term goal for each section of your Wheel, or even more. However it is probably best that you sift through your goals to establish up to one for each section only. This will allow your mind to adjust to the process and is easier on your brain than long and complicated lists.

You will find you can begin to practise by writing down on a separate sheet why you feel you desire to achieve each goal. Remember the benefits will determine your DESIRE for the goal, and clearly the benefits you most DESIRE are the best place to begin to work up your ideas into a full, clearly defined goal for the rest of the Night Book sections.

SECTION 5 – PROGRAMME PLANNER

This is the key to the Night Book, its most important feature. It is these sheets that have the impact and create the Gestalt and therefore your drive to achieve your goal, producing the correct attitude and a willingness to do whatever has to be done and getting on with it. Each part of the programme planner has an important function and must be understood and completed before the whole will come together and have an effect. Remember those final-year students who wrote down their goals back in 1953 at Yale University? Now you are going to do it in a very powerful and meaningful way.

Let's first look at the page layout before I explain each part in turn.

```
┌─────────────────────────────────────────────────┐
│  SECTION ─────────  DATE ─────────  LT □  ST □   │
│                                                   │
│  AFFIRMATION ─────────────────────────────────    │
│  ─────────────────────────────────────────────   │
│  ─────────────────────────────────────────────   │
│                                                   │
│  DESCRIPTION ─────────────────────────────────    │
│  ─────────────────────────────────────────────   │
│  ─────────────────────────────────────────────   │
│                                                   │
│  ┌───────────────────────────────────────────┐  │
│  │ PHOTOGRAPH/DRAWING                          │  │
│  │                                             │  │
│  │                                             │  │
│  │                                             │  │
│  │                                             │  │
│  │                                             │  │
│  │                                  SIGNATURE  │  │
│  └───────────────────────────────────────────┘  │
│                                                   │
│  PROGRAMME DATE ─────────  DATE ACHIEVED ──────  │
└─────────────────────────────────────────────────┘
```

One of these sheets should be filled in for each goal, believe me the routine you will adopt with this will work to real effect. The first line should name the Section of the Wheel of Life that the goal will affect most. The Date is the date you set the goal. LT and ST stand for long and short term, so tick off the appropriate box.

The Affirmation is best filled in after you have attended to the Description.

Description
Your brain needs a specific and clearly defined goal in order that the subconscious can get to work and play its part in bringing it into being. Just like the marksman you need an

accurate target. Too wide and the arrow has no real direction, firing off in the general direction of the target just isn't good enough – so be specific and clear in your description of your goal. For example, you may wish to set a goal for owning a new car. Simple programming for a new car isn't going to bring the results you require. You must decide, since there are thousands of options to choose from, which make and model specifically, which engine size, colour and specifications down to the finest detail.

The idea at this stage is to focus your thoughts on what you truly want in exact detail, so fill in these lines as best you can.

Once you get up and running with these techniques this almost becomes like filling in an order form. You send it off and sometime down the line it is delivered to you. Again, make sure you order what you really want. If you cannot find a description then you don't have a goal, you have an airy-fairy wish and that just isn't good enough.

Affirmation

Now, an affirmation is a single sentence (as short as possible) that encapsulates the description but has within its meaning the three 'Ps' – it is Personal, Positive and Present tense. Mohammed Ali's 'I am the greatest' was perhaps the best affirmation ever. He repeated this over and over to great effect as we have already looked at. Notice that it fills the necessary criteria required. It is Personal – it begins with 'I'; it is Positive – a statement of the direction he is heading in. (For example, to write 'I am no longer lazy' won't work because its focus is on the word 'lazy' and on what you have been, not what you are now. 'I am now full of energy' is much better.)

Third is that vital Present tense language, which reinforces the Gestalt in the brain. I recommend that you end with the

163

word 'now'. There are examples of general affirmations on page 50. Going back to the example of the car, above, your affirmation might read: 'I now drive a magnificent red 1994 Lexus 400.' The word 'magnificent' adds a bit of emotional content, highly recommended for any affirmation. Words such as 'happy', 'joyous', 'excited', etc. are useful to include. Do all you can to keep each affirmation as short as possible so that you can soon recite them all off at will. You can even sing them out to your favourite tune as you walk along or drive, or even when taking exercise.

It is vital that you write your affirmations down carefully because this is a crucial part of the Night Book routine.

Photographs or Drawings
Many people carry around with them photographs of their goals and aspirations. Looking at these builds excitement and desire. I have come across this with too many successful people to dismiss it. I am also aware of the power of subliminal advertising, which is banned because *'It Only Works.'* You will use something similar to programme your own brain to expect the outcome you desire.

Go out and find a photograph of what it is you are programming and be specific. We know that the brain loves colour, so do all you can to get a colourful photograph from a brochure or magazine. Cut it out and stick it onto the planner. If the box is not big enough then paste it on to the back of the previous page in your Night Book. Black-and-white photographs do work but they are slower in bringing results since colour will impact the neurons of your brain much more quickly. A drawing is useful when you are unable to obtain a photo – even a stick figure drawing will work, but do have an image. The routine that we will adopt with this completed programme planner works and works quickly to get you your goal.

Finally
Insert the date you intend to achieve your goal. Remember, think BIG, so watch that your logic isn't putting the date as far as possible into the future. The whole page is finally completed when you take your best pen and sign your signature over the bottom of the page. With this signature you are signing the contract. You mean business and you are making your symbolic commitment to the goal. This is a big moment, especially with all the effort you will have put into filling in the above information and finding an appropriate photograph or drawing.

Most Important of All – The Routine
Last thing at night, sit up, preferably in your bed, and go through the following steps with each of your goals set out on your programme planner. This is a must, indeed it is a vital process to go through. Make sure you find a way to do this. You may prefer doing it in a suitably quiet room before going to bed – it's up to you. It would seem, however, that getting into the same routine as you establish the habit is important. Your subconscious, for whatever reason, likes it this way.

- First – Read the description, its fine detail; after all you do have a specific goal.
- Second – Read your affirmation with enthusiasm as though it were already actually happening; just think how you would feel if that were true.
- Third – Look at the photograph with all the desire you can muster, this truly is what you want.
- Fourth – And this is what tops it all off. Close your eyes,

165

take a deep breath and imagine you are within your Editing Suite. Look up at your future screen, the one on the left, and see your programmed Future History once again. Really associate with it, what it will look like, feel like, what you will hear, the emotions involved, really be there with it.

• Next – Turn over the page and do the same steps (as above) with each goal until you are finished. Yes – you do this every night. This will establish the Gestalt quickly and tells your subconscious that you do indeed mean business and that you are prepared to do what has to be done till you achieve.

I also recommend reviewing your programme planners in the morning after you have programmed your day, before getting up and into it. You will find that within days of putting this into place that you begin to attract the people, places and opportunities that are required to get you there. You will also discover that occasionally you don't bother with it and put it off till the next night. Indeed you may even find your Night Book slides under your bed and out of your mind. When this happens everything slows down and you seem to be sliding backwards. There are no more coincidences and even doubt may set in.

However, something inside will get you going again. You will pick it up and get the kick-start you require. Almost immediately, the very next day, something in the way of an apparent coincidence tends to occur and you are off again towards your goal. Now, *'It Only Works'*, but YOU must make it work.

SECTION 6 – NOTES

This is simply a section of blank pages for noting down ideas when they come. You cannot know in advance how your subconscious will get to work to achieve your goals, so you must be ready when ideas start to come. They will come when you do not want them. You will most probably find that really good ideas and plans will come to your mind in the middle of the night or early in the morning and you must simply write them down. If you don't you may well forget them, especially those that occur in the middle of the night. Remember, never go to sleep without your Night Book and your pen or pencil by your bed.

SECTION 7 – DREAM LOG

It is very possible that your subconscious may use your dreams to throw up ideas, so again you have to be prepared. The idea here is to appreciate that if you wake up remembering a dream then there is probably a good reason. More often than not it won't be so obvious, so I recommend keeping a log of your dreams (see next page) and carrying out a study of them. It can be very revealing and more than interesting. Where would I be now if I didn't pay attention to the dreams I had way back then, which featured a house with a red roof by a river! The significance only came when I asked myself the right type of questions.

The trick, though, is not to analyse a dream just after it happens but to wait almost until the next night when you prepare to read your programme planners. The routine I suggest is to analyse it then, and go on to read your planners before going to sleep.

DESCRIPTION OF DREAM	
HOW DOES THE DREAM RELATE TO WHAT HAPPENED YESTERDAY?	**HOW DOES IT RELATE TO WHAT HAPPENED TODAY?**
HOW DOES IT RELATE TO WHATEVER ELSE IS GOING ON IN YOUR LIFE?	

So, whenever you remember the dream, be it in the night or early in the morning, write down a description of it. Wait until the next night before sleep, then remind yourself of the dream by reading the description before you address the questions in each box. Only by asking yourself the questions will you get an answer. It is amazing how ideas will emerge, or how the importance of an event that might otherwise have been missed will come to mind. Remember, you don't know how or when an idea will come. What you *can* be sure of is that once a programme is set up and running you will most certainly come up with ideas at the right time.

SECTION 8 – DAILY BRAINSTORM

The final section is in a sense an extra part of the Night Book, one that can be very productive and will in itself serve as a useful discipline. All you really need here is blank pages, but keep them separate from those in Section 6.

The idea here is to sit up in bed in the morning after you have programmed your day and reviewed your programme planner. Take a fresh page and write down 20 ideas that come to mind that would assist in reaching your goals. Don't in any way attempt to judge them, simply let your mind wander, let your creative faculties get to work and write down whatever comes to mind. Sometimes you will need to work at this. However, more often than not you will get into a flow of consciousness and it all just comes out in a stream of really good ideas. But do force yourself to do it.

This is a fantastic discipline, and over time you will be amazed by what you come up with. You see you really are a genius – you just don't know it yet!

Summary of Instructions

The greatest gift in life is the ability to think great thoughts and to have the strength to take action so those thoughts become reality in this wonderful and abundant world.

Complete your Wheel of Life at least every two months. This ensures balance in your life and points to areas where goals can be set.

AT NIGHT

1. You may add to your Gratification List and so thank your blessings for progress and achievement. This will reinforce your positivity and belief that you are deserving of your goals.
2. If required, analyse a dream with the help of your Dream Log.
3. Read your Programme Planners to impress your goal in your subconscious.

   a) Read your affirmation with enthusiasm and emotion.
   b) Read your description.
   c) Look at your photograph or drawing.
   d) Close your eyes, take a deep breath and imagine being in your Editing Suite in order to review your left-hand screen and your Future History again with feeling and emotion.
   e) Repeat for each goal.
   f) Go to sleep using the technique described in the next chapter.

IN THE MIDDLE OF THE NIGHT
Be prepared to write down dreams for analysis the next night; particularly write down any ideas that are generated while you are awake.

IN THE MORNING

1. Programme your day.
2. Read through your Programme Planners.

3. Write out at least 20 ideas that might help you to meet your goals.

DURING THE DAY

1. Take QRT, at least at lunch time.
2. Mentally rehearse before important meetings or events.

FINALLY

Act and pretend as though you are already a success and have already achieved your goal – and, of course, have fun.

My final piece of advice in the list above was to rehearse mentally. This is a technique that gives so many MindStore members their tremendous self-confidence and, like all the MindStore ways, they are not new. Everyone, I am sure, will remember Linford Christie standing with his eyes closed in front of the entire world before his Gold medal winning race at Stuttgart in the autumn of 1993. There he was with his eyes closed absolutely calm in all his majesty while all around him, in almost nervous tension, the other runners were attempting to loosen up while self-talking about their outcome.

Sally Gunnell was interviewed the night after she won her Gold medal at the same World Championships. She was asked how she felt when she came over the final hurdle to find her number one rival a full stride ahead. Her answer was magnificent and so inspiring to all of us who practise these techniques. She said how she had had to visualize that outcome for months yet still see herself winning. It is so important – let's join the

171

champions and get programming and mentally rehearsing – after all, *'It Only Works!'*

Summary

1. Make programming your day a way of life.
2. Start the day with a full 15 minutes of Quality Recovery Time and a programming session.
3. Remember, mentally rehearse before important meetings or events in your day.
4. Set aside the time to put together your Night Book and ensure that Gestalt occurs and that you achieve your goals.
5. Make reading your Night Book a way of life. Practise each night before sleep and in the morning after programming your day.

10

The Sleeping Quarters

A Good Night's Sleep is the Foundation of

Your Day

Perhaps the biggest stressor of all is the one known as *fear*. The Canadian motivational teacher Brian Tracy says that FEAR actually stands for False Expectation Appearing Real. He recognizes that FEAR is in the mind, that whatever one fears will exist in the imagination as an outcome or expectation which is so intense or compelling that it actually seems real. Certainly the processing of the expectation through the brain will trigger the stress response. The nearer the false expectation seems to be, then the stronger will the stress symptom be.

There are many fears that can strike the average human being. Classically we have a fear of ill-health, of death, old age, poverty, loss and criticism or rejection. Many confront the fear of failure and, for me, the big one: the fear of success.

The truth is that these fears exist only in the mind. People construct their own views and feelings about various outcomes from their own life experience and attitude. The more the negative outcome is played through the brain the more a person worries, the more this triggers the stress response and the more likely the person is to experience negative results.

Fears all too easily block success, happiness and achievement. Fear can lead to regrets over missed opportunities, it hides talents and skills, produces criticism and causes many to do nothing except watch life skip, oh so easily, by.

Constant worry, as you will be aware, causes major challenges to anyone engaged in it. I am sure that fear and worry have a major impact on our nation's well-being. Emile Coue found that by instructing his clients to repeat 'Every day and in every way I am getter better and better' as they took their medicine they automatically recovered better. What then must be the impact on someone's system when worry is a constant? We must guard against it – remember:

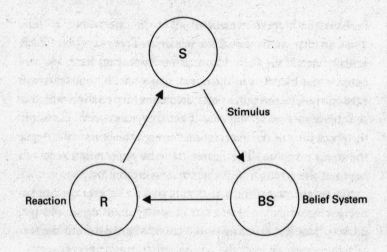

Delete that Programme and focus the mind on 'I can' and 'I will', on solutions and positive outcomes.

The solution is clearly in the mind. When I experience fear I have found that by standing up to it with positive self-talk and a constructive attitude it simply goes as I take action. By stepping into what you fear you find that it simply disappears. An example for me might be a steep slope that I am preparing to ski down. As I am not as good as I would like to be I can experience fear welling up inside, however as I actually move into position and take action my mind focuses on what has to be done and the fear simply vanishes. Remember, the brain can only process one conscious thought at a time.

The negative impact of fear will make you miserable – but only if you let it.

The first and best victory is to conquer self. To be conquered by self is of all things the most shameful and vile.

PLATO

I have learned to conquer my fear of ill health. This is a great victory for me since my hypochondria was debilitating. I worried sick about myself, I was preoccupied with my own being and was, in a sense, completely selfish. If you remember that you can only process one thought at a time then the solution will be simply to think about something else when fear tries to take hold. Since I realized that I was being selfish I began to force myself to think of others. By learning to focus on their needs, or observing their talents and skills, by becoming a much better listener I was able to take my mind off my worries.

Almost overnight I lost years of worry about my health just by becoming more engaged in what was going on around me. My experience of tackling this led me to realize that I worried more at night when in bed than during the day. This made sense, since during the day at work or play I had distractions and activity to keep me occupied, but at night I was left on my own.

On countless occasions I would wake up in the night only to get back to bed unable to sleep. Often I would actually wake up and immediately look at the clock before thinking 'Oh no, I'll never get back to sleep.' My bio-computer accepted the programme and that was it. It wouldn't be long before my mind turned to my health. Sometimes I would feel my pulse on my pillow. I would start to worry that something was wrong, I would turn round to find it on the other side just as strong

175

– 'Oh no, something is wrong.'

Just how many times did I find myself triggering panic attacks by focusing my mind on my breathing? Now, if you think of it nobody breathes consciously, we just do it, it all is taken care of at an unconscious level. But there I would be thinking about every breath and before I knew it I had to take each one consciously. I would start to panic as my breathing started to race. What a state to get into! It's funny now to look back on, but if you know what I am on about you will know what it is like. It is not pleasant.

Again, by deciding to conquer my thinking and through using Delete that Programme and thinking only positive thoughts with positive language I got rid of this great personal challenge. I am no longer a hypochondriac, I choose to focus on my blessings and strengths – and lo and behold I am far more engaged in living.

I felt then that techniques that could aid our sleeping and indeed improve our sleep would be worth developing and including in this book. Inevitably with the MindStore approach we will continue with the Architecture of the Mind and construct a room to sleep in.

The Sleeping Quarters

On reflection I realized that many people have no challenge in getting to and staying asleep. Many simply put their head on the pillow and they are gone. They claim to sleep soundly to awaken fresh and ready for the next day. However you sleep, I believe you will gain from introducing the MindStore approach.

On average we spend 30 per cent of our lives in sleep. We

understand that it provides rest and relief from our day, replenishing our energy for the next. For many it has long supplied them with solutions and ideas. The great religious books of this world, particularly the Bible, seem to be full of the importance of great ideas, visions and voices experienced in sleep. Our history is full of outstanding scientists and leaders who used their sleep time wisely.

I am particularly interested in this area. It seems to make sense that during the day our left, logical, reasoning brain has its domain, it's the dominant one usually corresponding to the Beta frequencies. At night while we sleep our right brain seems to have its domain through our dreaming, with the apparent increase in Alpha/Theta rhythms in our brainwave activity.

Many people just take their sleeping for granted, it's part of life. So they just get on with it and of course they enjoy it for what it is. Others at times find sleep a nuisance and would rather not bother, but of course they must, for however short a time they seem to get away with. I myself accept that there is overwhelming evidence for its importance both physically and psychologically, for our health and well-being, not to mention the role it plays in creativity and problem-solving. To 'sleep on it' is a powerful little phrase that has played a big role in the development of our world.

It would be sensible to make more of your sleep by first of all improving the quality and then developing the use of your mind while asleep. Inevitably with MindStore we will create a room and some tools to use there so as to bring about personal development during the night.

So, off the Central Hallway we will construct the Sleeping Quarters, a room you can use to sleep soundly and develop your creativity. Our expectation of this room is that it will provide a deeply relaxing, replenishing sleep, and as we wake

177

up naturally we will be full of the joys of life and ready with positive expectations for the day ahead.

The mental architecture includes a warm and comfortable room, decorated to your own preference, with a giant clock face set on one of the walls. Of course the central feature is the large, very comfortable bed.

The idea here is to access the sleeping quarters last thing at night by the Standard Entry Exercise – that is you will close your eyes and take three deep breaths while relaxing with each exhalation. You will then relax each part of your body, then imagine being on the right bank of the river. Go forward, enter your House by the Entrance Vestibule, have a shower in your Conditioning Gym and you are there, ready with positive expectation. This procedure will naturally take you nearer to the sleep levels, with a decrease in brainwave activity. Once there you will follow a self-control method of falling asleep.

For many the challenge with sleep is not falling asleep but getting up again in the morning. This can be a slow, reluctant experience setting up all kinds of negative programming in the bio-computer even before the day begins. Probably the vast majority of people use alarm clocks to ensure they wake up on time. We can choose to wake to the sound of music or of course our first 'hit' of news for the day, some will even wake to a cup of coffee or tea. Others feel the need for endless snooze buttons which are really a series of self-inflicted shocks.

The great Zig Ziglar, who is a giant in the personal development field, calls the alarm clock 'the opportunity clock', he so positively associates it with a fantastic day ahead. If you think about it the term 'alarm' has such a negative connotation, and for most that's exactly the state it induces in the morning. I soon realized that most people wake up before it goes off anyway, as though the subconscious gets to work, aware of everything, and saves them from the shock by ensuring they are awake to shut it off quickly or, even better, to cancel it before its time.

If the evidence from my courses stands across the nation then most do wake up before their alarms go off. I have also noticed that many people simply don't use them; they have learned to wake up just by telling themselves when they wish to do so. I remember as a child believing that if you knock your head on your pillow seven times then you will wake up at 7 a.m. (8 times for 8 a.m., 6 for 6 a.m., etc.). It's certainly the case that we do not need the 'opportunity' clock and can wake up at will.

Waking with the alarm has to have a negative side-effect. If, at the obvious level, it creates anxiety or a state of fright then we will start our day stressed. On the other hand, awakening from a dream state can create feelings of disappointment if seconds before you were about to experience something exciting or wonderful and you suddenly are shocked out of it. Does this set up negative expectations for the day? Who knows?

Back in the Sleeping Quarters, then, you will create a huge clock on one of the walls. It can be an analogue face (perhaps Big Ben) or a digital, but in order to impact the mind it will take up one complete wall. You will use this to set the time in your head before going to sleep.

The large comfortable bed you will use to help you to fall asleep. You will build an association between the idea of this really comfortable bed and a deep relaxing sleep. The more you use it the more it will produce the results you desire. The bed can be one you remember from some part of your life, perhaps childhood, a futuristic type of water bed or even a bed of roses. The idea here is simply to think of it as a warm, relaxing, comfortable bed.

The routine for falling into a deep relaxing sleep is as follows, and will be detailed further later in this chapter:

- Find a comfortable position in bed, then close your eyes and enter your House on the Right Bank by the Standard Entry Exercise (that is, three deep breaths while relaxing with each exhalation. Relax from head to toe, then imagine being on the right bank of the river. Go forward, enter your house, have a shower, then pass through your Central Hallway and on into your Sleeping Quarters).
- Sit on the large comfortable bed and look in your imagination at your 'Opportunity Clock' – remember, it takes up one complete wall. Imagine it spinning round till it stops at the time you wish to wake up. As you see it clearly in your mind say to yourself, 'At this time (e.g. 6.15 a.m) I will awaken and be wide awake ready for my day.'
- Then imagine getting into the large comfortable bed and follow the Pathway to Sleep.

Now it is important that you make your commitment to using the 'Opportunity Clock' by removing any other form of alarm clock. You will find you will wake up right on time, or even just before it. If you wake in the night, then before returning to sleep imagine the clock in your Sleeping Quarters and the time you intend to wake up.

I strongly recommend this as I am regularly travelling throughout the country staying at hotels in all manner of situations. I often have to rise at around 4.30 a.m. to catch the first flight out of Glasgow. I never use an alarm or an early morning call. *'It Only Works'*, and together with the Pathway to Sleep I do enjoy a good night's sleep every night.

If you think about it, waking up to an alarm means that the bell or buzzer goes off at any time in your natural sleeping cycle. If the responsibility for waking is passed to the subconscious then we can only assume that you will awaken naturally in tune with your body's rhythm, in a perfectly natural and healthy way. You will certainly feel better and may be surprised at just how well the technique works.

The Pathway to Sleep

Once you have the 'Opportunity Clock' set and you have got into your large, comfortable bed, you then concentrate on each part of your body, starting at the scalp and working your way slowly down to your feet. As you concentrate on each part repeat mentally to yourself 'I am falling into a deep relaxing sleep now' five times, then move to the next part of your body, relaxing it deeply and repeating five times 'I am falling into a deep relaxing sleep now.' You will find that you soon fall asleep.

So you fall asleep from within the sleeping quarters and will wake up naturally and on time. Like all the techniques, the more you practise it and make it a way of life the better you become at it and the more it just automatically works.

You may find that you do sleep better and wake up earlier than usual. If you do wake early you may feel refreshed but I strongly recommend that you do get up and straight into your day. I am a great believer that there are many good and wholesome things you can do with this 'extra' time.

The obvious thing to do is to get up and go for an early morning walk. There is something special about the morning air. If you are up before the rest of the world then you can really appreciate the magic that is the morning. Apart from enjoying the good fresh air, fully engage your senses: listen carefully you can often hear a symphony of sounds (especially in the countryside, but also in the city). The birds, insects, the wind in the trees, a babbling brook – it's all there to be enjoyed.

The special light in the morning can sharpen your sight. I particularly appreciate morning skies, especially in the city, where all too often our focus is on the ground watching each step. Look up – there's a whole new world of architectural wonder above your head. The country can provide brief glimpses of wildlife. And if you walk paying particular attention to your peripheral vision, it's amazing what you can notice.

A walk outside helps to set you up for the day. It can be so exciting to the positive mind. Just imagine what is in store for you this day. Clearly an early morning walk can provide the perfect environment for meditation or prayer. Why not have a go – *'It Only Works!'*

Just sitting up in bed and reading some inspirational book or a list of affirmations is also advised. You now have the ultimate in early morning reading: your Night Book and all those wonderful Future Histories. I often find that if I have spent time sitting up in bed in the morning and reading, when I eventually stop and put my reading down the time is exactly when I set my 'Opportunity Clock' for.

You could get up and engage in more involved exercise, stretching, warming up and enjoying a full aerobic workout. There is ample evidence now of the tremendous benefits of aerobics on health and well-being. After a full sleep there is no better way to start your day.

Dreams and Creative Thought

Once asleep we all dream, of course. Some people claim to be unable to remember them but it is clear to us now that we all do and that dreaming seems to be important. To a large extent dreams have resisted real scientific analysis although some great ideas have come from the likes of Freud and Jung. Dreams certainly seem to have a purpose, they are definitely interesting and entertaining, and they surely have a meaning.

It is accepted that when we sleep there are regular periods of deep sleep followed by a state when the eyes seem to flicker beneath the eyelids, popularly known as Rapid Eye Movement or REM sleep. It is known that we dream during REM sleep. Many great discoveries have been made in dreams. One Professor Friedrich Kekule discovered the molecular structure of Benzene in a dream of dancing atoms forming into snakes which swallowed their own tails while continuing to spin as if in a dance. On presenting his scientific paper he is reported to have informed his eminent audience of just how he first encountered his solution, and advised them 'Let us learn to dream, gentlemen.'

The great Scottish writer Robert Louis Stevenson is said to have encountered Dr Jekyll and Mr Hyde in a dream; Abraham Lincoln apparently dreamt about the assassination of a great president. Elias Howe, who invented the sewing machine, had worked for years on his great invention but could not come up with how to attach the thread to the needle. Then one night he dreamt that he'd been captured by spear-toting demons who ordered him to complete his machine immediately or suffer death. As they threatened him Elias suddenly noticed that their spears had a hole at the sharp end of the blade. He woke up and jumped out of bed realizing that he had found the solution.

183

He got to work immediately to finish the task. The hole in the sewing machine needle, as you probably know, is at the sharp end!

On the MindStore courses I play Mozart as the audience arrives and during rest periods. Apart from my own preference for his music I feel that it relaxes the crowd and for many triggers pleasant memories. I have always been fascinated by Mozart's great genius and particularly his creative drive. In a well-known letter he wrote:

When I am, as it were, completely myself, entirely alone, and of good cheer – say, travelling in a carriage, or walking after a good meal, or during the night when I cannot sleep, it is on such occasions that ideas flow best and most abundantly. Whence and how they come, I know not, nor can I force them.

The method of one of our greatest geniuses ever yet – and you and I know that this is how it works for us too. These special times of increased Alpha/Theta rhythms would naturally evoke right-brain activity, in Mozart and in all of us. I am sure you can all think of similar creative moments.

I often reflect on Mozart waking in the night with a great piece playing in his mind: the orchestra in full flight and the joy in his heart as he hears it for the first time. Just think, where would we all be now if he hadn't had the discipline and desire to write them down? Is it possible that some got lost in the depth of his inner concert hall?

What is certain is that countless works of art, scientific breakthroughs and wonderful inventions and ideas have got lost in the heads of those who did not have the discipline to write them down. It is clear we must be constantly on guard for good ideas.

How often have you woken up in the night with an absolutely fantastic idea, invention or business possibility? You get excited and enthuse about its potential, how it will sort out the challenge before you – but then you fall asleep before you can write it down. When you wake in the morning you cannot for the life of you remember it. It's gone, and probably for ever.

Or perhaps you have had a great flash of insight or a meaningful dream in the middle of the night. You start to think more deeply into it, bringing the logical, analytical faculties of your left brain into play, only to find that you now feel the need to put the idea aside: 'This won't work, don't be so silly. Go back to sleep, it's just a daft idea.'

I always ask my audiences for feedback during the course. Thousands and thousands admit that they never get their ideas at their computers, desks or work benches. They always report back exactly the same phenomenon that Mozart described. We seem destined never to get ideas when we need them but rather when we don't – when we are away from our work or the problem, walking the dog, on holiday, driving home or in our beds.

I remember Margaret Thatcher at the time of her resignation. She said that she had 'slept on it' the night before. Thomas Edison also stands out as one who used moments away from it all to find his solutions, particularly while asleep. I myself awoke from sleep on a number of occasions looking across a river to a house set in beautiful parklands – a house with a red roof. At that time I was searching for a vehicle to put these ideas together, and there it was. *It Only Works!*

Going to bed with paper and pencil ready for your night thoughts is something I strongly recommend you do from now on. Once you start to make all this a way of life then you will generate fresh ideas as you move forward. It is vital that you get into the automatic habit of writing these thoughts down. Remember, don't analyse them there and then; leave it till later in the day or even last thing next night.

In the previous chapter I introduced you to the MindStore Night Book System for personal success. It incorporates writing down ideas in the night and analysing your dreams.

From my experience of travelling the country and meeting thousands of people who desire to achieve more and lead a far more fulfilling life I have found that many have taken advantage of those times when they just cannot sleep. Has this ever happened to you? You wake up and then toss and turn but can't fall asleep again. I have come to believe that this is a signal that my subconscious doesn't want me to sleep for some (probably very good) reason.

The thing to do is to get up and leave your bedroom, go to another room in your home and explore possibilities. If you are musical then reach for your instrument and find out if a new composition is at hand. Get out your pen and paper and start to write. Maybe that letter you have always wanted to send to a friend now comes flowing from your mind. I've often got up and started to sketch and paint. Some people tell me that they have even used this time to tackle a little job around the house that they have been putting off.

What you will find is that when you have finished and you go back to bed you quickly fall asleep to awaken at your normal time feeling great and, of course, happy in the knowledge that you have done something useful in the night.

REMEMBERING DREAMS

For some of us every night in bed is like a trip to the Odeon (except that the show is far better than anything produced at the cinema!). Others never remember their dreams although they accept that they must have them. There are many stories about Thomas Edison and his creative mind. I came across one about a pad he kept by his bedside. He used to write on it:

I am about to fall into a deep relaxing sleep and on awakening I will remember a dream.

Later he developed this to 'I am about to fall into a deep relaxing sleep and on awakening I will find the solution to...' and then he would add the problem or task before him.

You will find that as you repeat the Pathway to Sleep phrase 'I am falling into a deep relaxing sleep' if you add 'to find a solution' or 'to remember a dream' you will tend to wake up to find it there before you.

I myself, using 'Edison's Pad', have invented a special reading tool that improves my reading pace considerably and has helped me come up with some great ideas for some of MindStore's most important tools and techniques. Again, *It Only Works!* Why not have a go?

As far as the interpretation of dreams goes, then of course their meaning would seem to be very subjective. I include a Dream Log in the Night Book System, explained in the previous chapter, that will assist in this. There are, of course, countless books that have been written on dream analysis and you may gain some insights by studying them, although I am more inclined to feel they are personal and that any individual's dream symbology can only have meaning for them. There are a number of groups around the country who meet to share their dreams.

You will have noticed how some dreams seem to relate to events of the day before. I often wonder if by remembering

187

them my subconscious is attempting to draw my attention to their importance. On the other hand, most people I've talked to have experienced precognition in their dreams. Take the dream of an old school friend, neighbour, colleague or family member. Next day they turn up in your life – perhaps physically, perhaps on the phone, by someone mentioning their name, etc. This is quite common. Many people I have met have also had warnings in dreams of accidents, deaths and disaster. *Déjà vu*, many think, first exists in a dream which is then suddenly 'flashed back' for a split second when we encounter the real place, face or sound.

I use my sleep time to assist my own personal growth and understanding, and I recommend the same for you. Get into the habit of sleeping with pen and paper ready, just in case. Use your Night Book. As Mozart said, you cannot force great ideas, so be on your guard. Be ready and marvel at your undoubted creativity.

EXERCISE 6: THE SLEEPING QUARTERS

In this exercise you will again enter your Foundation level and your House on the Right Bank by the Standard Entry Exercise before leaving the Conditioning Gym to create your Sleeping Quarters off your Central Hallway.

Finding a comfortable position in your chair, close your eyes and begin breathing in a regular and slow manner. We will now begin to focus your mind and body on relaxing into a healthy state of being. Once again, as I mention each part of your body concentrate on it and focus your thinking on producing relaxation.

Take a deep breath and relax...take another deep breath
and relax...take a deep breath and again relax...

My scalp is relaxed, I feel my scalp relaxed... My
forehead is relaxed, I feel my forehead relaxed... My
eyelids are relaxed, I feel my eyelids relaxed... My face
is relaxed, I feel my face is relaxed... My tongue is
relaxed, I feel my tongue relaxed... My jaw is relaxed, I
feel my jaw relaxed... My throat is relaxed, I feel my
throat relaxed...

My shoulders are relaxed, I feel my shoulders relaxed...
My arms and hands are relaxed, I feel my arms and
hands relaxed... My upper back is relaxed, I feel my
upper back relaxed... My chest is relaxed, I feel my
chest relaxed... My lower back is relaxed, I feel my
lower back relaxed...

My abdomen is relaxed, I feel my abdomen relaxed...
My hips are relaxed, I feel my hips relaxed... My
thighs are relaxed, I feel my thighs relaxed... My knees
are relaxed, I feel my knees relaxed... My calves are
relaxed, I feel my calves relaxed... My ankles are
relaxed, I feel my ankles relaxed... My toes are relaxed,
I feel my toes relaxed... My soles are relaxed, I feel my
soles relaxed... My heels are relaxed, I feel my heels
relaxed...

Take a deep breath and relax...

I will now imagine that I am in a very special place of
relaxation... I fully pretend that I am there...I will give

189

myself a short period to engage fully in this and enjoy it [30 seconds]...

Take a deep breath and relax.. I will now adjust and imagine that I am standing on the river bank, the river is behind me and I am facing into a wonderful landscape...

I can feel my feet on the lush green grass...overhead the sky is deep blue and the air is fresh with the scent of the meadow...I can hear the sounds of the wonderful landscape before me...

In a moment I will stand within my shower and cleanse away any current negativity...

I now enter my showering area and turn on the flow in order that its imaginary cleansing action can commence...I pretend to feel the warm spring waters run through my hair and down over every inch of my body, draining away mental fatigue and restoring vibrant life in its wake...

I now imagine the bright sunlight reaching deep within, filtering out and washing away all my limiting and destructive attitudes, particularly my negative thinking today...

Readjusting and turning off the shower I now step out, instantly dried and fresh with positive expectations...

In a moment I will create my Sleeping Quarters, which

is entered by a doorway off my Central Hallway... It will be used for sleeping soundly and for developing by creativity...

I now leave my Conditioning Gym and enter my Central Hallway, with its images depicting times from my past when I have been at my very best... I now create the room that will house my Sleeping Quarters... I decide on its shape and the height of the ceiling...now the decorative features, colours and lighting... On one of the walls I place an attractive clock face that covers the entire wall... And now a large, comfortable bed...

By entering my House on the Right Bank last thing at night and setting the time at which I wish to wake up on the clock face, and by falling to sleep by the Pathway to Sleep, I will fall into a deep relaxing sleep before waking up on time feeling wonderful and in perfect health...

I have now created my Sleeping Quarters for sleeping soundly and developing my creativity...

I will now leave my house and return to the river's edge... I feel the lush green grass beneath my feet... I will shortly count from 1 to 7 and gradually adjust to come out of this healthy state of deep relaxation... 1...2...3...4...now beyond the midpoint, when I open my eyes I will be wide awake and revitalized both physically and mentally...5, I begin to adjust my body...6, I prepare to open my eyes...and 7, I open my eyes, wide awake now, both physically and mentally alert.

191

Summary

1. The brain can only process one conscious thought at a time, so continue to use positive self-talk when facing up to your fears.
2. Fear exists only in the mind. Learn to take action, to step into what you fear and discover that it no longer exists.
3. Do away with your alarm clock and get to work with setting an 'Opportunity Clock' in your mind within your Sleeping Quarters.
4. Use the Pathway to Sleep and ensure a deep relaxing sleep each and every night.
5. Take advantage of waking early to get up and enjoy a walk or to read a motivational book.
6. Keep your Night Book by your bedside for noting down ideas that come from sleep.
7. Learn to study your dreams in order to gain deeper insights and harness much more of your creative capacity.

11

The Other Rooms

Part of the MindStore courses include, as you might expect, a number of other rooms in the House on the Right Bank. Each contains powerful tools which you can use for specific purposes. Indeed, you are always at liberty to create new rooms in your House on the Right Bank as your own self-knowledge and development throw up new possibilities. Once you make MindStore a way of life, you will develop your own ideas – ideas that I would never have thought of (believe me, many, many of our members have).

You can add rooms once you become proficient with what you have now in the way of MindStore tools, or you can add immediately to your mental architecture if you want to improve your performance in, for example, sport, the arts or your pastimes.

I myself built on my inner landscape a bowling green at the edge of a garden I had created. This was some years ago when I had an interest in bowling and played at least once a week with friends. Although I enjoyed the company and competition I was never seriously committed to doing what is required to win tournaments. I was a reasonable player but certainly not in the top flight, nowhere near it.

Practising in my imagination, where I could play perfect shots every time, I was able to 'groove' success into my subconscious. I would play there, where time didn't exist, every night. I remember I had been moved by the story of a Vietnam prisoner of war who apparently 'played' (in the privacy of his imagination) every single shot of a full 18-whole round of golf every day during his horrendous captivity. He would play each make-believe round from different angles and positions. He would take hours and this allowed him to preserve his sanity while all around him the madness and deprivation of war raged on.

On returning home to the US many years later he eventually got back to his golf club and played his first real round in six or seven years. To everyone's amazement he played the round on level par – better than he had ever done before. He of course was not surprised, since in the confines of a tiny and crude cell he had learned the importance of controlled imagination and DESIRE, BELIEF AND CERTAINTY.

I can tell you that within six weeks of using my bowling green on the right bank I was selected to play at county level. I tell you, *it only works*. You can have a golf course, tennis court, ski slope and endless other possibilities. Practise when fully relaxed, develop your commitment to whatever level of performance you desire and observe how you improve, especially if before each competition you take time out for QRT and a full mental rehearsal. I wouldn't dare claim that you will win all the time, because sport is really about participating whatever the outcome, but you will enjoy it more and be better than you would otherwise.

Artists have reported back to me that they have constructed an inner studio where great works are shaped in their mind and completed in the finest detail before being presented to the real world. Musicians also report back improved concert performances by adopting this idea. They practise perfectly and just before the performance they enact a full mental rehearsal in the Editing Suite, framing the standing ovation of the crowd and focusing their energy – they then do indeed perform to their very best.

There really is nothing new in MindStore. One of the great stories from history is that of Nicola Tesla, the great champion of the development of electricity. He designed powerful yet perfect generators, but his method – which led to breakthroughs in his field – involved passing over responsibility for creativity to his subconscious. He would begin with some rough drawings and then, relaxing and stimulating his imagination, he would pretend to be in a workshop in his mind. At an imaginary testing station he would set up the prototype and turn it on so that it was working.

His genius was to leave this prototype 'running' in his mind, telling himself that he would return in two days' time to check for wear and tear and any other fault in its operation or design. When he returned to his inner workshop he would find that adjustments were required. Once the changes in design were in place he would repeat the two-day test run. On each return visit he'd make the necessary adjustments until he had the perfect electrical generator. His job then was to transfer it to the real world via his own pristine engineering drawings and by supervising all phases of production. Every one of his finished works were perfect in every detail.

It has always been this way. Both brains are required for success. The future exists in the imaginary world of our mind. It has to exist there first before becoming reality. What kind of images have you been contemplating? You now have the tools and understanding to make the difference. Learn to control your imagination and create a perfect Future History. The programmes will be running anyway, so why not join me and create the world you truly want?

Take the action you must take with dignity, strength and

courage in order to find the solutions that will help us all to live happier, healthier and more prosperous lives.

Suggested Reading

Richard Bandler and John Grindler, *Frogs into Princes* (Real People Press, 1979)

Tony Buzan, *Use Your Head* (BBC Books, 1974)

George S. Clason, *The Richest Man in Babylon* (Signet, 1988)

Dr John Diamond, *Your Body Doesn't Lie* (Warner Books, 1979)

Mark Fisher, *The Instant Millionaire* (Pan, 1990)

Timothy W. Gallwey, *The Inner Game of Golf* (Pan, 1979)

—, *The Inner Game of Tennis* (Pan, 1981)

Jerry Gillies, *Money Love* (Bantam, 1978)

Robert Heller, *The Super Managers* (Penguin, 1984)

—, *The Super Chiefs* (Penguin, 1992)

Napoleon Hill, *Think and Grow Rich* (Wiltshire Book Co, 1937)

Napoleon Hill and W. C. Stone, *Success Through a Positive Mental Attitude* (Thorsons, 1960)

Maxwell Maltz, *Psycho Cybernetics* (Wiltshire Books, 1960)

Andrew Matthews, *Being Happy* (Media Masters, 1988)

Dr Joseph Murphy, *The Power of Your Subconscious Mind* (Thorsons, 1963)

Norman Vincent Peale, *The Power of Positive Thinking* (Cedar Press, 1985)

Anthony Robbins, *Unlimited Power* (Simon & Schuster, 1986)

David Schwartz, *The Magic of Thinking Big* (Thorsons, 1959)

Index

Further information on the courses Jack Black and MindStore provide for the business community, the general public and for children is available from MindStore, MindStore House, 2/4 The Wynd, Cumbernauld, Glasgow G67 2SU. Telephone (0236) 729830.

Super Confidence

Gael Lindenfield

We all envy confident people for being open, secure, relaxed and successful. But did you know that confidence is not something you have to be born with? It is possible to learn confidence, and if you need a little help along the way - particularly if you are a woman - this is the book for you.

You can learn how to:

- Cope with anger and criticism
- Communicate effectively
- Deal with difficult people
- Stand up for yourself
- Get what you want out of life

By working through *Super Confidence* you will be able to bring your own inner confidence to life and gradually build up your own self-assurance. Then you can stand tall and bring out the best in your relationships and your work.

'Sensible, practical, and exceedingly useful'

CLAIRE RAYNER

Even Eagles Need A Push

David McNally

Young eagles do not learn to fly until they are pushed out of their safe nest. Until they learn to soar, they do not discover the privilege it is to have been born an eagle.

This book is about your success, your happiness, your work and your dreams.

It is about the power to create what you want for your life.

It is about discovering a true sense of purpose, the contribution that only you can make to the world.

It is about courage, determination and commitment. And it is about love and appreciation.

Most of all, it is about rising above the turbulence of these uncertain yet exciting times to chart a meaningful course for your future.

Do It!
A Guide to Living Your Dreams

John Roger and Peter McWilliams

We all cherish at least one dream – a heart's desire. Moreover, it is a fact that most of us do have the time and the ability to fulfil our dreams – if we put our mind to it. Unfortunately, we spend all our precious time and energy on other things, often completely unrelated to what we really want to do. What is it that makes us procrastinate?

The answer is the comfort zone – the old, safe, practised thoughts, responses and actions we feel comfortable with. Pursuing a dream involves ways of thinking and acting that are outside the boundaries of this comfort zone. But how can we overcome such a problem when we probably aren't even aware that it exists?

This book provides the answer.

- recognize your comfort zone and learn to go beyond it
- discover, or rediscover, your dreams
- choose which dreams to pursue
- work out practical solutions for achieving them

As the authors say, 'LET'S GET OFF OUR "BUTS".'

So stop making excuses, and start living your dreams!

Success Through a Positive Mental Attitude

Napoleon Hill & W. Clement Stone

This international bestseller reveals the thinking of two highly successful men - who want to help you match their achievements! To ensure your own success they encourage you to take a fresh look at your life and to start by seeing yourself as the most important person alive. This is just the first step in a process which can transform NMA (negative mental attitude) to PMA (positive mental attitude). The other vital steps towards success include:

- having a definite purpose - choose your own direction
- developing personal initiative and self discipline
- using creative visualization
- employing organized thinking and concentrating your effort
- time - and money - budgeting and
- plenty of enthusiasm!

From job satisfaction to good health, PMA will help you ensure you make the most of all your opportunities. And there are plenty of successful examples to illustrate that these principles really do work.

Food Combining For Health

Doris Grant and Jean Joice

Food Combining for Health is the international bestseller that has improved the health and vitality of thousands.

Also known as The Hay Diet, it is based on Dr William Howard Hay's eating system, devised nearly 100 years ago. Many have found that it has helped to alleviate arthritic pain, digestive disorders, ulcers and obesity as well as many other health problems.

Food combining is easy. Simply by keeping starch foods separate from protein foods in your daily diet, foods can be digested more easily, and your general health improved. Doris Grant and Jean Joice have taken a fresh look at Dr Hay's teachings, and they offer lots of practical advice and suggestions including a comprehensive recipe section to show you how easy it can be to begin food combining for life.

'I am sure that today I couldn't cope with the work I do without the diet.'

SIR JOHN MILLS

'Within just four days my weight had dipped effortlessly.'

BARBARA GRIGGS, *VOGUE*

Super Confidence	0 7225 2651 2	£4.99	☐
Even Eagles Need A Push	0 7225 2759 4	£6.99	☐
Do It!	0 7225 2695 4	£7.99	☐
Success Through A Positive Mental Attitude	O 7225 2225 8	£5.99	☐
Food Combining For Health	0 7225 2506 0	£4.99	☐

All these books are available from your local bookseller or can be ordered direct from the publishers.

To order direct just tick the titles you want and fill in the form below:

Name: ....

Address: ....

　　　　　　　　Postcode: ....

Send to: Thorsons Mail Order, Dept 3, HarperCollins*Publishers*, Westerhill Road, Bishopbriggs, Glasgow G64 2QT.
Please enclose a cheque or postal order or your authority to debit your Visa/Access account-

Credit card no: ....

Expiry date: ....

Signature: ....

- up to the value of the cover price plus:
UK & BFPO: Add £1.00 for the first book and 25p for each additional book ordered.

Overseas orders including Eire: Please add £2.95 service charge. Books will be sent by surface mail but quotes for airmail despatches will be given on request.

24 Hour Telephone Ordering Service For Access/Visa Cardholders - Tel.: 041 772 2281.